WAKE UP

FROM LIFE

Recognize Your True Self

By Lili Apine

Acknowledgments

My deepest gratitude to Brigita for her loving support and presence as well as to Jason for the valuable editorial advice.

Contents

Preface

Wake up from Life: Recognize Your True Self provides a direction toward the recognition of one's true self for those within whom a deep pull towards the truth in its deepest sense is alive. Also those who are interested in learning the perspective that has revealed to a regular human being by waking up to its unchanging nature will find value in here. Everything written here should not be perceived as thoughts and opinions of a person, rather an understanding arisen from the beyond-personal perspective. Obviously, it is expressed through the subjective consciousness of an individual; however, hopefully as its impact decreases all written here is minimally distorted by the mind and is clear and easy to understand.

I have attempted to write in a completely open and honest manner, as otherwise the point of this book would be lost. When it comes to deep existential matters, undistorted experience is of utmost value. This book has been created because an aspiration arose to express what is seen from this perspective. At the same time, based on experience as an individual who was actively seeking truth, it's clear it is worthwhile learning the viewpoints of other human beings living today who have come to see their true being.

This way of expression will not be suitable to all and is not intended so as it is direct and therefore doesn't show much empathy towards affections to different aspects of life. However, by no means should it be perceived as indifferent or deprecatory towards all worldly and human experiences, as the aim of this book is to reflect the understanding of this reality arising from the beyond-personal perspective as clear as possible.

Wake up from Life includes essays, a collection of best Q&A's written on the blog http://www.nothingeverhappened.org as well as offers extra content and expanded, in-depth presentation of the nature of existence, and practical methods, guidance for self-inquiry and meditation.

The Path

It is always interesting to hear individual stories of the path towards spiritual awakening - which stages of development and what interesting events have been experienced. A chronologically unfolded life story indeed helps an individualized mind to understand the process of awakening better at least conceptually and believe in the possibility of one's own awakening, as well as to see similarities between the story teller's and one's own experiences.

I must add these past events and seeming development is no longer perceived as personal, as I see now they haven't actually happened to me. They were experienced within me. I cannot even fully rely on their realness, as all that I know about them are memories which are not my direct experience of the now. And memories are nothing more than thoughts which always takes place in the now. Therefore, they are by no means indisputable proof of "real" events that have taken place at some point. If they are not now, then also when they seemingly were, they were not fully "real" because the absolute truth is that which is always here, always permanent. Respectively, all that is changing is not the absolute reality.

Unconscious Beginning Turns into Seeking

I have always felt internally that this body and "material" world is not all there is, and my being reaches much further out than this. I believed in this from childhood. It was of course only an intuitive feeling, and there were no conceptual framework for this. It was limited to knowing that something higher exists, overarching to what we can perceive through our ordinary senses. It was supported by some experiences which could not have been explained within the generally accepted framework of this reality. At least then they couldn't have been explained.

An active interest in reality outside of a strictly materialistic outlook of the world appeared when I was around 13 to 14 years old. My mother owned various books with an esoteric orientation. I started to read them, and from the very outset they seemed fascinating, my interest was sparked. Initially the information which I digested with such great appetite was more of a superficial nature – reincarnation, life after death, karma, astral worlds, working with energies as well as personal development topics.

It is very possible that this interest in such topics at quite an early age is at least partially related to over-sensitiveness, reserved character and inability to fully socialize with peers due to insecurity. Thus, an increased interest in such books which promised much greater and more significant reality behind this tiny and insecure person certainly brought some comfort and opportunity to hide in a much more pleasant world of ideas.

I also remember that during adolescence this ordinary, materialistic reality seemed so depressing, gray and emotionally cold that I just could not accept that it was all this existence can offer. I thought it was not worth living in such a world. Some moments of joy in no way outweighed this grim, harsh and intolerant world. Of course this age corresponds to a traditionally difficult stage of growing up. However, I certainly don't want to state that such a perspective was wrong and distorted due to a biochemically sensitized perception. No perspective at any age through the prism of a person is objective; and therefore none of these experiences are less real.

Strange Sensations and Experiments with Various Disciplines

One uncommon experience that appeared at quite an early age already, which I remember well, was a frequent feeling of light pressure on the upper part of my head as if I had put a hat on whose edges lightly pushed against the skin. I didn't pay much attention to that, and I didn't know the cause for it. Later these feelings disappeared. Only years after when they showed up again, that time more distinctly and along with other sensations, I would find out the cause. According to an understanding of Eastern traditions and philosophical systems such or similar sensations are side effects of the activation of head or crown chakra. It also has a connection to the awakening processes of kundalini energy. Meditation practitioners sometimes observe such sensations.

At the age of 14 or 15 I participated in seminars where under the guidance of a gifted teacher we trained our ability to sense beyond our ordinary organs of perception – telepathy, gaining information without using our rational mind, feeling energies, seeing auras and consciously leaving the physical body. And it indeed brought results. Afterwards I didn't continue training these abilities for very long, however, as I simply didn't have motivation strong enough. It just didn't seem necessary for me.

Then gradually more deep and meaningful books appeared. They not only pointed to different realities and ways how to manipulate this reality by consciously directing one's flow of consciousness, but also provided explanations on existential matters. These were mainly Eastern philosophies.

I must add that it is very possible it only seemed that I gradually gained access to books with more meaningful content. It could be that information of various depths and complexities has always been around; yet, one simply doesn't notice that part of all information available which doesn't correspond to one's stage of development.

During that time I also started practicing meditation. Now of course I know that I had a vague understanding of what meditation is. Yet, that is completely natural because as it seems evolution is an inescapable feature of all things in this reality.

At the age of 16 I started attending hatha yoga classes. Also regarding this I can now conclude that at that time I knew very little what this practice is for; although I had never viewed it as purely physical exercise. Regular visits to a yoga studio had another auspicious impact. It provided access to wider information as lectures on various related subjects were organized at the same yoga studio. When Peteris Klava (a life-long seeker and reanimatologist) started giving lectures there, it can be considered an instant when I finally accessed immeasurably more valuable knowledge. He introduced me to teachings and philosophies that provided satisfying answers to most fundamental existential questions. I was fortunate to hear about such Eastern teachings as, for instance, Dzogchen, Advaita Vedanta and also about various ancient and more recent enlightened beings. This in turn gave the opportunity to learn more about these sources of knowledge on my own. I am infinitely grateful to him for this.

For a few years I was enthusiastic about lucid dreaming. Such an interest was spurred by repeated unintentional waking up within a dream state as well as several experiences during a half-sleep half-awake state. It is possible to gain such a state where during the sleep one suddenly recognizes that it is a dream by applying various methods. This state can be used for different purposes; however, I was interested in consciously exploring dreaming in order to recognize my true nature. Tibetans call this dream yoga.

At the same time in parallel to delving into deeper teachings I was still practicing various methods for self-improvement and thought realization. I attended seminars for healing and working with energies. Although I write about it as if it is of little value, it all has its own significance along the path, and if it has no real value then at least it shows that the truth is not to be found there.

For instance, still at the age of 25 I attended several practical seminars in which shamanic methods were taught and practiced. These were diverse exercises – leaving the body to consciously float above it, traveling into previous lives and various healing techniques. It was interesting for a short period. Regarding the exploration of different aspects of my own individualized consciousness this method allowed me to see and at least to some extent release some deeper layers of accumulated redundant ideas and emotions. However, I realized that such an exploration and delving into the depths of one's own subconscious mind, with an intention to heal and release the nods created by past events, could continue infinitely. This repository is inexhaustible, it seems.

Apparently this reality expresses itself in a way that focusing attention towards a certain direction itself creates new objects of exploration. I concluded that if it's not some "nod" or an accumulation that greatly disturbs the current role to fully express itself, or if it doesn't overly agitate the mind, thus preventing the recognition of truth, then it is not worth spending time on it. Furthermore, these seminars were designed for participants to create a new identity or an idea of the "I" by establishing an affiliation to a certain community, as well as to gain new attributes like name and others. That obviously did not align with my inner desire to rid of anything redundant as during that phase I didn't want to acquire anything anymore. All I wanted was to clear all falseness away.

One Wish Only, the Final Stretch

Approximately around the same time when these explorations were taking place my aunt who was interested in similar matters suggested looking at the videos of Mooji, which are available in great number on the internet. Mooji has recognized his true nature and widely shares his perspective with truth seekers. I call this moment a breaking point in my path of seeking as finally I could receive clear knowledge, clear teaching on that which interests me the most from a live teacher who can provide an answer to the most essential question, 'Who am I?' For a year and a half I listened and watched his *YouTube* clips intensely. At the same time thanks to *YouTube* suggested videos I learnt about many other contemporary teachers, awakened beings related to non-duality traditions.

During that time I experienced quite radical changes in the perception. An increase of awareness of the totality of everything and love towards everything started to take place rather rapidly. It is not easy at all to describe it using words. It is a total change of the position of perception. All is now observed from an absolutely peaceful, neutral, yet, compassionate and loving point of view, not anymore from the position of the person. This observer is aware of an individualized person played out here, its thoughts and actions. Simultaneously changes took place also in the "physical" perception. The vision became as if clearer, the colors brighter; although it wasn't an optically measurable increase of sharpness of the vision. It is a different kind of clarity. The physical sensations of the body were also not left unchanged. They became lighter and felt different. The dynamics of these changes can be compared to a gently sloping curve that grows in height slowly with several separate more rapid jumps.

For quite a long time and increasing in intensity I experienced a feeling as though I was behind a glass wall separated from all else. Every experience was accompanied by a feeling that although I could see, hear, taste and sense all that's perceivable, I could not fully reach any particular object. It felt as though there was an invisible, insurmountable wall between me and the perceivable object. For instance, when looking at a beautiful nature scene, I had a feeling that it was not possible to wholeheartedly enjoy and "touch" it for real. The same sensation occurred with music, food and contact with other people. I couldn't merge with it all or fully enjoy it; therefore, a distinct feeling of the illusory nature of all the surrounding started to appear. Nothing seemed real as I couldn't find the core being, the source of these surrounding objects. It stopped at the moment when I came to see that I have no borders and all takes place within me. When I ceased directing my attention to the "external" world or perceivable objects and stopped looking for an independent substance for it all outside of me, the feeling of separation disappeared and I came to see the source of all, which is not different from my true being.

For some time oscillating changes were observable – one moment there was a blissful state and love towards all, in the next instant they were completely gone and I had returned to full identification with the person. The mind had become restless and rebellious again. At times like that I felt trapped in an unbearably small cage in a desperate situation. Laughing and crying without reason was a common phenomenon, which still, although more rare, can take place. It's very likely a way how deeply buried emotions and beliefs are released when mind is being cleared of these accumulated remnants of past.

Simultaneously with an increase of awareness, the expressions of ego or the illusory "I" were noticed more distinctly and quicker – as a thought or desire to be special, appreciated, a desire to achieve something. There has been an uninterrupted vigilance to spot and "neutralize" such thoughts and feelings. Mooji provides wonderful suggestions regarding this. Listening to him developed within me an ability to spot instantly any means that ego uses to try and maintain its autonomy.

At a time when a strong identification with the person still pervaded, yet, the interest in worldly matters like cultural, entertainment events, hanging out with friends and reading books had completely gone, I was often overwhelmed by a sense of being at a dead end. The mind frantically tried to find some activity to keep it busy with, to gain more time and delay the end of its ruling. However, none of these activities gave much satisfaction. I felt as if in absolute darkness on what to do. Everything that was happening in my surroundings as well as my own thoughts and emotions seemed unbearably fake and stilted. All that appeared in the mind was instantly recognized as another way of the mind to draw the attention away from the essential by forcing it to go towards mundane, worldly objects of this phenomenal world. And because such immersion into worldly objects could not happen anymore, yet, I hadn't recognized my true nature yet, my mind felt as though it was cornered. I wanted to not exist; however, it had nothing to do with the death of the physical body.

During the same period I developed some health issues. I was hospitalized due to spontaneous pneumothorax or a rupture in lungs tissues. It happened suddenly; and it was also relatively quickly healed not leaving any significant consequences in the body. Traditional medicine couldn't identify the cause; yet, it coincided with a time when I had for a few years already practiced each evening pranayama breathing techniques designed for awakening and rising up of kundalini energy. Possibly it was holding of breath for too long and insufficiently deep exhaling that caused such an incident. However, this incident is worth mentioning for a different reason. While I was at the hospital, a complete surrender and full trust in all that was happening took place within the individualized consciousness, without fear, leaving only love towards everything. Quite possibly health problems possess a transformational function in this reality.

About half a year after that a sudden shift created the most significant overturn in the perspective so far. While I was sitting at the desk in my workplace, suddenly a moderate sting of pain appeared in the body. The pain was not strong, and it lasted only for a brief moment. Usually one doesn't pay attention to small discomfort like that. However, in the same instance I recognized that I am not this body – I am everywhere and this body is located within me. It was irreversible. The identification with the body has never returned.

Thus the perception of my own boundaries had changed. No boundaries, spatial or time, were left. I look at the horizon and know that I am also there, or all that I can experience (hear, see, smell, taste or touch) takes place in me. Seeing my true being, it becomes clear that it is not located within time. Time takes place in it. If I compare the feeling of my deepest sense of "I" at some point in childhood and what it is like now, I see that it is identical. In my deepest being no changes have taken place. That which constantly changes here are merely waves on the surface that in no way impacts the deepest being. And it is amazing to see this, as it frees me from fear of death because it becomes absolutely clear that death is simply impossible for my true being, as it has never been born. Instinctive reactions, however, remain in threatening situations. They are necessary for keeping this dream body alive.

After another half a year I went to visit Mooji in Portugal where his main residence is located. The community of Mooji's followers offers possibility for truth seekers to live for a few weeks among them meanwhile engaging in fulfilling practical errands of the community. The decision to travel there was made quite spontaneously. It fulfilled without any obstacles although at the point of decision I didn't know yet how I would acquire necessary funds.

Once I got there, a completely different world revealed itself. Life in Latvia was forgotten for a while. The time spent there seemed long, yet, not because of boredom, but due to intensity and abundance of inner processes that took place. It was incredible of course to meet and talk with Mooji in person after one and a half year of intensive viewing of his live and recorded videos. However, here listening to his words had very little significance. The presence and undivided attention to the recognition of one's true self speeded up greatly the increase of awareness and decomposition of the mind's accumulations.

During my stay in Portugal I underwent unpleasant feelings, discomfort that relates to the resistance of ego or idea of "I" to the processes that inevitably lead to a radical decrease of its power and influence. I experienced sudden and bright moments of full clarity of the illusory nature of this reality and my person. Also flashes of the recognition of my true nature as *the ever-present Consciousness* were experienced. However, the ordinary perception always returned. Unprecedented sensations within the body were experienced as well. For instance, at one time during meditation quite suddenly great warmth and lightness appeared within the chest creating a sense of relief and liberation. It was as though I had never truly breathed until now.

I was different when I returned to Latvia. A few months later an aspiration to continue watching/listening to Mooji's records dissipated. I simply had a feeling that it was no longer necessary.

After a while the seeing had stabilized, and the ordinary, dual perspective no longer returned. Initially after recognizing my true nature the mind out of a habit attempted to appropriate the new understanding as if its own. However, such an attempt was unsuccessful as the seeing matured to a point where the strongest concepts were already released and the mind had become much quieter.

During this period of approximately 3 years (from the age of 24 to 26) the desire to socialize was minimal. Most of my time I spent alone as I felt nothing from this world could bring me joy. I strongly felt the senselessness of everything here. It wasn't disparagingly, though. Unconditional love towards all kept on increasing. I simply didn't want to participate in it. I was interested in one matter only – to recognize who I am. However, half a year after visiting Mooji this perspective changed quite rapidly and I felt a pull to be in society, to enjoy expressions of this reality, to be in a relationship without seeking anything, simply enjoying this existence.

This return to willingly take part in this relative world didn't have any adverse impact on being aware of myself as the permanent Consciousness. On the contrary, this awareness kept on becoming increasingly distinct. There were no fluctuations left in the seeing. Everything was firmly seen from an ever-lasting, ever-present, unchanging peace. Yet, still until this very moment the clarity of the seeing keeps on slowly increasing, subtly, but noticeably. Some spontaneous instants of even higher clarity keeps appearing, which indicate that this seeing is still slowly maturing.

This pull towards enjoying society again is in no way a step backwards or a distraction from the essential. It is a natural change in an individualized consciousness that has been striving towards merging with its "source" for a long time, and finally having seen the true nature of all existing, feels great love and pull to enjoy interaction with different aspects of itself and other beings.

Throughout these years there have been many unusual and interesting experiences, which cannot be portrayed briefly. Retrospectively assessing this path, it seems that the most significant events and circumstances have been auspiciously designed for the Consciousness to recognize itself as the

Consciousness in this form. However, looking at this from the perspective of the Absolute, these circumstances or efforts have not been the cause for awakening. All expressed in such a way because awakening was already taking place, and the dream was simply adjusted to explain and make sense of it.

Oddities of Awakening in This World

It is no surprise that after a complete shift of consciousness from personal to absolute it may not always be easy to keep operating in this reality in accordance with its rules. The dream goes on and the role one is playing must be played out regardless of being awakened. Yet, it is not quite right to say that it is "hard" to keep on acting in this reality because without an active ego and knowing I can't be harmed, life can actually be enjoyed much more fully than before. I will mention some temporary or permanent oddities that were or are experienced after having firmly come to see my true nature and returning to fully engaging in this world.

Initially when I had reached certain clarity in seeing the non-existence of my boundaries, it brought some surprising sensations. At one time while being in a public place I experienced that people who were at least four meters away from me suddenly felt as though they were too close to me, violating my personal space. I got used to it rather quickly; although sometimes I can still experience this. Sometimes seeing the movements of someone else closely located, naive amazement arises about not being able to sense the feelings created by the bodily movements of the other person.

At some point I noticed my mind had become significantly slower in thinking. It lost its acumen. Also the memory is sometimes deceived as there were incidents, not that rare, when memories of a fragment of some conversation or an event had been completely lost. Others would remind me of the existence of those past events; yet, there were no signs of them within my memory. Certain details that seemed significant I could memorize quite well; however, matters that didn't seem important looking from the new perspective, I simply could not keep in mind. This phenomenon can be observed in an ordinary mind as well. Yet, the difference is that the perspective on what is important and what is not important has changed. This applies not only to details, but also to quite relevant world events that I often easily forgot. It truly is a change of focus from the past and future to here and now.

Interaction and communication with others, for a while, had become more complex because of a slow perception due to which it was often hard to grasp what others wanted to convey. Meanwhile it was also burdensome for me to be able to express myself clearly and quickly enough. At the time I was working quite an intellectually demanding job that also required communicating. While I was still working there I felt as though I was no longer suitable for the particular job. I didn't have any interest in the work I was doing anymore. It simply felt meaningless. Therefore, I began looking into different possibilities to earn a living. I saw I was becoming unfit for the particular job not only because of a loss of interest, but also because I couldn't fulfill the necessary functions as good as previously due to my slow mind, sluggish perception and unreliable memory.

These features are fluctuating, though. As of now these "disturbances" have lessened, or I simply have gotten used to them. There are other aspects that might have a greater impact on making one's expressions socially awkward. I realized that I have always been a bit socially inadequate. However, in some ways it has gone even further after awakening. The ability to understand subtexts decreased, and often I found myself clueless on what was considered an adequate action in a particular situation, or what had to be said that would correspond to socially accepted norms. Moreover, it was and still is difficult to see hidden or not so hidden intentions of the individual I am commuting with.

Only when my girlfriend shared her observations and we assessed how I see a particular situation in comparison to how she and others most likely see it, this "inadequacy" became clear. Until then I didn't have a clue that I am not seeing something fully or that I am not acting in accordance with the expectations of others. My partner is still in a way a human interpreter for me. She explains what someone meant by what they said or what kind of a reaction is expected in a given situation.

Nevertheless, differences in perception of the matters of this world between me and my girlfriend or others are not because I am unable to see things accurately. There is no objective, correct world. Each individual mind is a whole world. Therefore, these differences in perception simply indicate that our experiences vary. We experience different realities. After awakening it is quite natural that these differences can sometimes become truly stark, not only fundamentally, but also in the details of how we interact. Yet, if someone directs my attention to the fact that I might have misunderstood something, at that moment it becomes part of my reality and I must accept it and act upon it if necessary.

I still experience stress, emotions and pain; yet, none of these cause suffering, none of these can hurt deeply or for a long period of time. It is in some ways like being an ocean. Stones on the surface cause ripples; however, these ripples cannot penetrate the peace that lies deep down. Thus if negative emotions do arise, they swiftly vanish. They are not seen as something undesirable that one must get rid of, though. They flare up and disappear without a trace.

While this human form exists, individual characteristics remain. Thus, outwardly it may look as though there is a person within this being; although it is rather an empty façade that sees itself as the ever-present Consciousness in which such a form arises. Characteristics and expressions of this form can change of course. They become gentler. Also tendencies and habits remain. However, they are more like inertia from previous actions. If new habits are formed, they are completely peaceful in nature.

What Everything Is About

After revealing I am not a human being, everything becomes so beautiful. No contradictions remain. There is only that which is. To that which is many names such as *the Consciousness, the Absolute, God, the Supreme* and *the Being* have been given; yet, no one can accurately express it in words. Only the Being is. And this Being is *self-knowing*; it knows itself. And it is the only true *Knowing*. All other knowledge is merely a false interpretation. "The human" is nothing more than an idea that has temporarily seemingly appeared in the Being. The thought "I am an individual" arises when one's perspective is limited and attention focused on this narrow viewpoint.

By bringing attention back to the source of the observer or by defocusing attention, this dream, which we call "the world", is dispersed and then vanishes. Objects are an interpretation of the perception. No proof can be found of the existence of any object. Also "I" and the world are objects created by interpreting this sea of impressions that are played out in the Consciousness. Even saying "created" is not quite right as nothing has truly been created. The Consciousness is seemingly temporarily lost within itself by mistaking its own shadow to be "the other".

To believe in one's memories is similar to accepting a truth from a stranger passing by without any verification what the stranger has said. Any belief arises due to a lack of knowing oneself. All mundane knowledge of this world is believing in unproven ideas. And in order to strengthen these beliefs, people also believe ideas about the evidence which supports these beliefs. Someone believes in matter, someone believes in gods; yet, in all cases these are merely ideas. Know what you are, and you'll know everything, or, to be more precise, you'll be the Knowing itself.

Everything that is experienced is a perception. Due to not knowing oneself, our perception, which is formed by seeing, hearing, touching, tasting and smelling, generates an illusory interpretation of reality that acts out as a mind's activity by creating ideas, concepts and memories. The idea of "I" is the only one that causes suffering. And this suffering seems as real and strong as one believes in the idea of "I" and other objects because both are being experienced within the same dream.

Where is my body? Everything I experience is the perception. And a cluster of these perceptions we interpret as the physical body. However, no one has ever directly experienced one's physical body. All perceptions appear in the Being. And, when they are realized as they are, without any mistaken interpretation, all perceptive experience is blissful and infinitely beautiful.

The Being is absolutely peaceful. The mind is unrest, as it is a collection of mistaken interpretations of the perception. It is unrest, as it doesn't know what it is. There is no peaceful mind. The mind is merely a concept similar to all other ideas. It is not possible to speak about the mind as of some sort of substance, as it is merely a cluster of thoughts or interpretation stream of the perception.

The Being, when recognized, is blissful, absolute happiness. The Being does not take place in time. Time is changefulness of the interpretations of the seeming perception that always take place in the eternal now. We seem to experience such a phenomenon as time only due to a continuous flow of changing interpretations of this reality; yet, it all takes place in the now. Nobody has ever experienced the future nor the past. The past is a concept that has been created by believing in memories, which are nothing more than thoughts, which are interpretations of the perception. The future is also an idea that arises from the thoughts about possible next variations of the perception. Even to say "present" is misleading, as the usage of this word indirectly points to the existence of the past and future. Only the Being is.

A Return to Primordial Peace

That primordial peace in which everything appears is accessible to everyone. However, that which prevents us from being aware of it, is a full identification with our current roles and a complete merging into worldly events and
situations. Most likely everyone has felt and been in a state of absolute calmness and fulfillment for at least an instant. Until such a state became a permanent background for me out of which everything is experienced and observed, these kinds of moments appeared mostly when I was alone or with someone whose presence does not require taking up a role. They were also experienced in meditation when the mind had become quiet and attention brought back to its source.

The best illustration for this primordial peace is in the context of lucid dreaming. If one has ever experienced waking up within a dream and realizing that it is a dream, not the awake state, then one is also familiar with that stark difference between a regular dream state and a lucid dream. In the regular dream state only dream events and dream identity exist, full merging and a belief in realness of what's happening takes place. And because of this a strong emotional involvement arises. Whereas being in a lucid dream state and therefore, knowing it is merely a dream, brings great peace and freedom.

In an instant when it becomes clear that what's being experienced is a dream, finally an ability to fully enjoy the surrounding events with an ease appear knowing one's inviolability and immortality. In that state not only is there no fear from the impermanence of the surroundings, there is even a desire to play and willingly expose the dream reality to a dynamic change with deep enjoyment. It is possible only because an implicit awareness of one's unchanging, eternal being is present. It is important to add that during lucid dreaming the "I" is not identified with the person having the dream - the one who is at that moment peacefully sleeping in a bed. There are no memories or interest toward that.

In a way it is similar to playing tension full video games. If the player had to fully forget that he is actually located in his own room and had to identify with the role of someone within the game who runs around under constant death threat conditions, it would most likely be perceived as a nightmare. Exactly this awareness of the fact that nothing can actually hurt me whatever danger takes place within the game, results in enjoyment and a desire to play and act being free from the restriction of the fear of death.

Similarly, this so-called awake state reality is a temporary phenomenon which one fully believes in, thus losing the awareness of one's own true nature or that primordial peace. It is not a mistake, though. What could really be a "mistake" looking from the absolute perspective? In the absolute reality the word *mistake* has no meaning. In this reality an event and some characters attitude towards it appears simultaneously. None of these - the event or an attitude towards the event - are truer nor more objective than the other.

There is no value in looking for reasons why has this forgetting of one's true being occurred, sinking us fully into this phenomenal world. When looking from the absolute perspective, from the unchanging, eternal Being, there is no meaning to the words *cause* and *meaning*. Only in this relative world do they have a use. Let's return to the dream state analogy to illustrate this. I have experienced, and I'm sure others have too, that within a dream in which I am not aware of the fact that it's a dream, all seems incredibly real and self-understandable. There is no doubt of its realness and nothing surprises. However, after waking up and recalling the dream, it is not possible to comprehend the logic that was experienced within the dream with the mind in its awake state. Furthermore, often it's nearly impossible to describe it to others. Similarly, what happens within this awake state reality seems completely rational and self-understandable only within this subjective reality.

Some of those who have recognized their true nature, however, do provide a reason why the Consciousness has become "lost" within its own projections. The most common explanation provided is that the only way how the Absolute can experience itself is through a separation and from losing awareness of itself. They say, if this seeming separation would not have happened, the Being would be completely amorphous, homogeneous and without any movement and possibility to gain any experience. Nevertheless, it is not knowledge based on a direct experience. It is only an assumption provided by the human mind that is not capable of comprehending the lack of space and time and to whom the lack of movement associates with boredom and can even raise a fear. Therefore, while we perceive through this relatively limiting form, we cannot truly know or imagine reality beyond its expressed state.

Expressing in this reality creates great enjoyment for the consciousness that no longer experiences a dual state, however, still preserves an individualized form. Any movement creates deeply blissful love and compassion towards those aspects of itself expressed in other forms that suffer due to not knowing themselves. Experiences of many of those who have recognized their true nature affirm this. After recognizing one's true nature increasingly, yet sometimes stronger, sometimes less distinctly, a contact with various objects, alive or not, also feeling one's own body brings great enjoyment. This enjoyment doesn't compare to anything else. It is difficult to express it in words. Perhaps it could be compared to the feeling of satisfying a thirst after being very thirsty, without experiencing the thirst itself.

Sooner or later primordial peace recognizes itself within every form. Can it be promoted by the efforts of a conscious spiritual practice of the seeming individual? In accordance with how I see it, an interest in spiritual matters and a desire to practice is more like a symptom that indicates approaching awakening. This statement obviously is not pleasant and is almost unacceptable for the seeker because it has not recognized itself yet as the timeless and space-less unchanging, ever peaceful Consciousness. It sees itself as an individualized, separated being that is under an influence of "external" circumstances and is surrounded by "external world" objects. Therefore, a thought that it doesn't possess its own free will and it cannot influence events with its own mind, is unbearable. The mind simply cannot accept such an idea because at the very base of its own construct of the world is the idea about "the human". Yet, the idea of "the human" is impossible without the concept of free will. There is no human without free will. And in the end it turns out the human being indeed has been only an idea which one had temporarily believed in.

Regardless of how attractive it is to discuss different approaches one can adopt to promote awakening, in the instant when one recognizes their true nature, it becomes clear that a human cannot wake up; only the

Consciousness can wake up from a temporary delusion that it is a human being. And then it is not an individualized consciousness anymore.

Thus there is no one that could enlighten. This aspect also points to the critical threshold during the process of awakening. While there is someone who strives to be enlightened, awakening cannot take place. Only at the moment when the idea of an individual being is seen as illusory, it is possible to recognize one's true nature. In this instant the foundation of the illusory perception irreversibly cracks; however, the seeing becomes clearer only gradually. A misleading perception, which has been reinforced for years, accumulated beliefs and notions, which have been accepted without questioning, slowly fade away. My experience so far shows that the deepening and increasing sense of clarity of the seeing never stops at least while this form exists. There is no testimony on what happens after the cessation of this form.

The non-existence of free will and the illusion of an actual individual evolution, however, don't mean there is no value in a conscious striving towards spiritual awakening. If the interest is genuine, it couldn't be stopped just by hearing that it won't be the cause for awakening. There is not much to do with knowledge that the free will doesn't exist, as the understanding of it cannot influence future behavior and decisions in any way, even if it looks as if it has impacted it.

We Live in a Reality of Paradox

Speaking of the ordinary perception of the world, it is quite right to use words such as *dream, illusion* or *apparent*. However, by using these words, I certainly do not point to its worthlessness or irrelevance. Rather, I emphasize the fickle and impermanent nature of this world, as well as that all that can be perceived here is not self-sustained, or that this world is not the final, fundamental reality that doesn't depend on any other. And anyone can verify this by having a fresh and concept-less look at this reality and by analyzing what is truly seen. Even without such experimental looking and analyses of this moment's experience it is quite rational to conclude that this changing reality can exist only because of some ever-permanent reference point. Otherwise if the observer who perceives everything were not stationary, it would not be possible to detect and perceive any movement because without a permanent, stable reference point a change wouldn't be seen and experienced as a change.

Furthermore, "I" cannot be anything that I can perceive. It can be my expression, but in my essence it is not me because all that is observed (also the body, the mind, thoughts and feelings) are objects. Thus, I will never be able to see myself, my true Being. I can only be it. At the very moment when there is anything to point to - I am this! - it must be recognized as only a phenomenon. That what I am is the one experiencing the phenomenon. I have no form, characteristics, location, age or any other limiting property that can be attributed only to the phenomenal world.

Speaking of this relative world and absolute reality, one has to accept the following paradox - although when looking from the absolute reality this relative world is merely a temporary appearance without its own independent existence and real substance, still it is not insignificant and despicable. Even though it is a transient dream, the characters of this dream do not doubt the severity of all happenings, and, therefore, they experience it in all seriousness and enjoy and suffer accordingly. Thereby, all that's taking place here is and isn't at the same time. It is, because it is being experienced very realistically and with all the resulting consequences. And it isn't because it is highly transient; after a moment it no longer exists. The reality of this relative world does not exist on its own. It appears only within a subjective experience or within the reality created by the individualized mind. One must add, essentially there is no fault in this seeming reality. It is not that everyone should hurry to wake up from it.

At this moment an objection might arise - is there not a single objective reality then? If there wasn't any, there would be no consensus at all on this perceivable world among separate minds. Furthermore, an idea might arise that perhaps all other humans are only a creation of my own mind, and, therefore, they are not real. Indeed, there are many commonalities among people in the way they perceive the "external" reality. Also some more or less differing aspects exist; yet, the commonalities are great enough to conclude that it is the same "objective" reality we are talking about. However, this correlation does not point to many human beings living in one world, rather it indicates towards one consciousness within which many beings are manifested. All the minds don't share one world; they share one consciousness, thus resulting in many similarities within each experience. Francis Lucille has provided a great analogy for this by comparing this with a round tower which has windows next to each other facing all sides. "The light of consciousness" that is looking through all of these windows is one; yet, each window, an individual mind in this analogy, shows a different angle. There is a certain overlap in the landscape for neighboring windows; however, there are differences as well.

Why aren't other human beings the product of my own mind if I have no proof of them also having their own consciousness? This solipsistic question is based on a misunderstanding that "I" as an individual possess a mind. Looking from such a perspective it really could appear that there is no evidence from our direct experience that other beings are not merely a product of my fantasy or projections. However, the individual itself is the same thing as the mind (in the wider interpretation of the mind, including thoughts and all perceptions), and this individual mind appears in the Consciousness, which is always and everywhere just one.

The mind does not create anything; it couldn't create or imagine other beings. It simply doesn't possess such autonomy. The mind doesn't have an independent existence, a core, which anyone can verify just by trying to follow the thoughts, ideas and memories to see where they come from and to see what it is that produce them. The mind is an appearance in the Consciousness just like everything else that can be experienced - surrounding objects, other beings, the feeling of self as an individual, thoughts and emotions. They all appear in one Consciousness. The source and essence of each phenomenon is this Consciousness.

Thus, it can be said that absolutely everything possesses consciousness; however, it is not very accurate. A more precise statement would be that everything appears in one Consciousness.

Time is in the Mind

It is not easy to think about time because the thinking itself takes place in time. It is almost impossible to comprehend some phenomena while being under its influence and not being able to take a step back to see the context in which it takes place. Therefore, it can seem even a bit torturous to discuss time because the thinking mind cannot see itself from aside and thus with great effort tries to provide an explanation for itself. This in turn points to the nature of time as well as its relation to the mind.

Time is a construct of the mind, or it is experienced only in the mind. With the term *mind* here one should assume its wider meaning – not only thoughts, but also any kind of experience and perception (seeing, hearing, touching, tasting, smelling and other feelings). That what I actually am does not take place in time. Time is experienced in me. In fact, it is not possible to talk about it as though it was a separate phenomenon. It is nothing other than a byproduct of the mind's dynamic nature, its continuous changefulness. The past and future of course don't exist and have never been experienced. There is only the eternal now in which thoughts about the past, which we call memories, and the future, which never arrives, are experienced.

Outside of this relative world time is an empty sound without meaning because it truly doesn't exist. Scientists have long been discussing the unbreakable relationship between matter and time (in this case though, not taking into account that matter has never been found). And indeed objects are not imaginable without time or vice versa. However, it is much simpler than it may initially seem. Time and matter are simply two concepts that represent the dynamics of all that is played out in this reality (i.e. the mind). In fact, these concepts are created by the mind trying to explain itself to itself.

All that we experience, in this perceivable world, can only be observed because we see it from a completely still viewpoint that doesn't take place in time. Only because the observer is in a static position, can he perceive changes taking place. From this it follows that anything that is changeful is not my true nature. I am the absolutely permanent, ever-present screen or the Consciousness in which all worlds are being manifested.

Enlightenment is not an Event

For a long time the word *enlightenment* to my understanding had a mystical connotation. I believed it to be a mysterious event that expressed itself as an outwardly visible, extreme and sudden change in a human resulting in an achievement of absolute happiness, a gain of a super-human ability to influence this reality as well as the end of ordinary functioning in society. However, as one can guess, there are various misunderstandings and false presumptions in this. It is quite important to free oneself from these myths by gaining at least a conceptually close understanding of what *enlightenment* is. Of course an understanding on the level of the mind is not even close to true experience. However, it seems that for many westerners an intellectual understanding is essential for further awakening processes and direct experiences to take place. Also for me it was a crucial part of the whole self-recognition process, which still continues.

Various words are being used for this, most common being *enlightenment*, *awakening* and *realization*. The word *awakening* has become more popular in recent years among the truth seekers as it sounds less ambitious and for the time being is more or less free from mistaken associations. According to my understanding the word composition *self-recognition* is accurate, as it points to the fact that nothing new is being gained. That, which is, always has been. It has only been temporarily "veiled".

The definition of *enlightenment* in one sentence could be: the recognition of one's own true nature or being. However, obviously more detailed explanation is needed here, as much as is possible using dual linguistic means. First of all, a human being, a person or an individual cannot achieve enlightenment because enlightenment is to see that in my true being I am not this person. The person and its reality are being experienced, it takes place in me; yet, it is not my core being. It follows that enlightenment can be defined also as freeing from mistaken identification with a person, a human being.

Secondly, nothing can be actually achieved as my true nature has always existed. One could say, it has always been enlightened. Simply a mistaken interpretation of perception had taken place, which resulted in taking this apparent role as the real "I". Enlightenment is not really an event in the ordinary meaning of the word *event* because nothing really happens - in the absolute level no changes have taken place, no changes could ever take place. Changes can be seen as changes only in relation to something that remains static; yet, the Absolute only is. It is everything. Therefore, *change* as a concept can exist only within this relative, dual world.

However, self-recognition within this apparent reality is experienced as real changes on all levels of perception - increasing blissful peace that permeates all experiences, seeing one's personality as a constructed idea, which now causes laughter, as well as feeling everything else - people, things - as part of oneself. It is almost impossible to describe it in words so that someone who hasn't experienced it can imagine it accurately. Yet, it can have no effect on the outward appearance and functionality of life. A job, habits and friends - outwardly all these can remain as previous, or changes can be gradual. Then again, others can experience extreme changes in all matters of their life.

Then what really happens at the moment or process of awakening? In brief, the mistaken perspective deteriorates revealing an increasingly clear awareness. It is difficult to say it more precisely. It is awakening similar to what we experience each morning. The dynamics can vary, though. Based on what I've heard about the experiences of others and from my own, it most often manifests itself as a gradual, progressive process with some separate instantaneous shifts in the perspective along the way. It is very possible that Rupert Spira is correct when he argues that the recognition of one's true nature is instantaneous. All further processes are only an integration of the new perspective, a gradual deterioration of incompatible beliefs and notions. A lot can be said about these further processes.

In general the change in perception is radical. After it the experience of the reality is not "same as it was previously, only more loving and peaceful". It is a complete shift of self-perception - a shift from the personal, separated and fearful perspective to the ever-present, ever-lasting and unchanging Consciousness. Thus, everything in this reality is seen very differently. There are moments when less active state occurs when awareness of the body and this person completely disappears leaving only the peace of the primordial Being, absolute indivisibility. It is truly a blissful stateless state.

Joy, unconditional love for all, happiness and peace arise as by-products as one increasingly clearer and brighter recognizes their own true nature. It is like the feeling of happiness as one returns home. All conflicts and contradictions disappear. It is undoubtedly seen that I am one with all "other people" and not only people. All seems dear and beautiful. As I mentioned earlier, in my case it didn't change in a single day, and it keeps on becoming clearer and brighter.

That Which is Beyond the Consciousness

Is there anything beyond the Consciousness, or is there an even higher state then being awakened? After self-recognition one's consciousness in a way is still characterized by dynamism because a passive activity (being conscious) is still taking place. In a way it still is a dual condition because, although it is seen that I am everything, individualized experiences still take place. That which is everything still is in an expressed state; it experiences diversity and vitality within itself. This can be compared to lucid dreaming – although I see that it is only a dream and it takes place in me, it continues to play out.

Whereas the "state" about which it could be said that it is beyond the Consciousness, only is. It doesn't experience itself in any expressed form. No perception, no activity takes place. Each night we are in such a stateless state. It is deep sleep, which we have no recollection of. All that is possible to say about it from the perspective of the awake state is that it is incredibly pleasant and we are happy to return there every night. We also know that a true rest during sleep takes place only because of the deep sleep phase. It is not possible to say much more about it not because it would be an interruption in existence, but because no experiences as well as no mind take place there that could have registered an event that it could later recall. That which is everything was in an unexpressed "state", blissful peace.

After one has recognized their own true nature, the interruption of this dynamic consciousness can take place not only in deep sleep, but also during the awake state. It is recognized by absorption into blissful peace. Eastern cultures refer to it as *nirvana* or *samadhi*. During awake time this "state" can be experienced for a mere instant, a flash or longer, or it can be achieved during meditation. Yet, I must add, it is not correct to say that it is possible to *experience* it because it is the purest being in which all experiences have ceased their existence.

In order to linguistically distinguish these two "states" - seeing one's true nature while still observing its dynamic expression and the pure, unexpressed stateless state beyond the Consciousness - some awakened beings use words

Consciousness and *Awareness* respectively. These words are necessary only for the sake of convenience of communication of course.

Love is Pull Toward Home

It is possible to talk about love roughly in two planes – love toward all existing and love toward one particular individual. Although one could regard the first type as more pure and fundamental as it does not depend on existence of a certain object, also in the case of second type the source of love is the same, and in its deepest sense the striving is for the same thing. Yet, in the second type this striving manifests itself through some definite form of existence.

Striving for love is an aspiration toward the re-union with one's primordial being, toward awakening as the ever-present Consciousness. Longing for a complete union with the other in partnerships reflects the deeper lying natural desire to re-unite with the Consciousness or the Absolute. And it is possible only by losing the illusion of an independent "I" or losing oneself.

This aspect points to the limited expression of love in relationships among two people that don't want to renounce identification with their individualized roles yet. There is pull towards oneness; yet, it cannot happen all the way because too strong is the tendency to maintain the belief in one's autonomy. A pull toward two opposite directions exists, thus making one experience conflicting feelings.

Love is home. It is our most natural state when we know ourselves as the Consciousness. And it is the only criteria that could be applied in this relative world in order to determine if something is proceeding toward the "good" or not. Respectively, is there love? Does it increase?

Love is not some kind of a special energy. And to speak about it as an emotion is to greatly disparage it. It is not quite correct to speak about it as an appearance either. Rather it always is like an aroma of our true nature; yet, it is temporarily veiled or lost because of an apparent separation.

By itself love is always unconditional. Various conditions that create disappointment or dissatisfaction with the other in partnerships are consequences of not knowing one's true nature as well as having accumulated misleading notions and beliefs about the world. By believing in oneself as a person, unavoidably conflicts with the surroundings arise.

The Meaning of Life

The human mind has been traditionally engrossed by the question of the meaning of life or the meaning of this existence if we consider ourselves to be immortal beings that aren't limited to one life only. The expression *the meaning of life* these days is sometimes used with an ironic tinge as if showing that there isn't any greater meaning.

Yet, to answer this in a way that there simply is no meaning would not be quite right. Life or existence is not meaningless. Simply, on an absolute level of truth such a concept as *meaning* does not exist; therefore, the question itself is based on a wrong assumption. All is as it is because that is how this expression takes place, without any reason or cause. Causes and effects are observable only when looking from a dual viewpoint, from a perspective that arises from believing in oneself as a separate person.

However, it is possible to say something about the meaning of this reality in the context of the absolute truth. As mentioned earlier, this temporary delusion of the Consciousness taking oneself to be an individual is a way how the Absolute can experience countless expressions in itself. Without it no relationships, no experiences would be possible. Therefore, the ability of the Absolute to experience itself within itself could be regarded as the meaning of this existence.

There are people who claim development and evolution to be the meaning of life. However, it is rather an expression of this existence not the cause for it because for development to be of any significance there should be something less developed in comparison to something that is higher. Yet, such categories can be viewed as real only within this relative world while we consider ourselves to be separate, independent beings that are slowly traveling along a timeline and changing. At the moment when one comes to see that the true nature of all existing is absolutely permanent, beyond time and always flawless, the meaning of concepts *development* or *evolution* can be found only for characterizing the dynamics of this relative world.

Nevertheless, while everything is perceived through the prism of an individualized consciousness, causes and effects are experienced; therefore, also the meaning and significance of various processes and whole life are experienced. Each experience is real. There is no experience about which we could say that it is not real. One should be aware, though, that every experience is a subjective projection of the Consciousness. Thus, while a phenomenon – life and some "I" that lives it – is perceived, also the meaning of life can be experienced. However, only each specific mind can formulate it for itself in accordance with its particular seeing.

What is it That Reincarnates

One of the assets of this reality that has taken a firm place in many people's comprehension of the world is reincarnation. I could have skipped this concept altogether because it is a phenomenon just like any other appearance in this perceivable world that is manifested within this cosmic dream. Therefore, a detailed exploration of reincarnation does not provide answers to the deepest existential questions. However, at least I, when I was still looking for the answers, was interested in understanding what it is that reincarnates if there is no individual, independent being or a soul in its traditional understanding.

Evidences on rebirth from life to life in this reality can be found quite a lot. Stories of bright and remarkable memories and unexplainable coincidences can be heard from various sources. Thus, there is a place in this reality for the phenomenon of reincarnation as well – not in all minds, but for sure in a significant part of them. Nevertheless, how should one look upon reincarnation when it includes such individuality confirming attributes like personal growth, distinct characteristics and experiencing consequences of one's previous behavior? What does it suggest?

The Consciousness is one, and it experiences itself through an infinite number of individualized viewpoints. That which is transferred from one dream episode to another or from one life to the next is a cluster of beliefs, strongest characteristics and tendencies that must be played out in order to be freed. These individualistic sets of features can be called "souls". Yet, all of it is played out in a single Consciousness; therefore, no independent beings exist that incarnate, later leave the body and repeat it many times.

Such a journey of the seeming individual is played out in the Consciousness; and it is real for the particular point of perception while a belief of oneself as an autonomous person exists. Therefore, when dealing with the matters of this relative world, like some highly disturbing aspects of the personality or difficulties in relationships, delving into the scenarios of past incarnations in order to entangle them can be useful in some cases.

How to Recognize Oneself as the Primordial Peace?

When an intellectual understanding about what awakening is and what it is that must be recognized has been gained, quite a natural next step is to implement it. A question might arise then – how to do it, how to recognize oneself as that primordial peace? Unfortunately the mind must experience disappointment regarding this because there are no instructions that could be useful to the mind. The mind is asking "how?" Yet, there are no answers to *how?* questions because it is not the mind that must do something. After all, the recognition of one's true, eternal nature can take place only when the mind itself has been overcome.

By *overcoming the mind* I don't mean destroying it or leaving it fully behind. As don Juan said to Carlos Castaneda the crown of *the tonal* (all perceivable, this world, the mind) must be taken away from it. However, at the same time *the tonal* must be protected because without it this dream could not take place. There would be no life. By taking away the *tonal's* lead, *the nagual* (the pure Being which is the source of everything) becomes "visible" or is recognized. At the same time in order to gain a greater possibility to recognize *the nagual* or one's eternal, unexpressed being, *the tonal* must be made balanced and healthy or strong enough in a sense that it doesn't show any excesses, negative tendencies or a complete lack of self-confidence and willpower.

The above-mentioned indicates that in cases when an individual shows a significant lack of self-confidence, doesn't possess a strong inner core or shows some essential imbalance, it can be of value to primarily carry out practices and get to know teachings that allow making the human expression stronger within this relative world, even if they don't provide the absolute level of truth yet.

Nevertheless, when great enough stability in one's expressions as well as an intellectual understanding about the nature of the reality have been gained, it is not worth delving into countless books that provide descriptions of various methods and traditions anymore. Beyond this point it is merely a mind's procrastination because the mind doesn't wish for the recognition to take place. It is interested in maintaining a continuous bustle so that the primordial peace wouldn't reveal.

How to realize this recognition then? There is no answer to that because it is revealed by itself. However, while no other way is possible, the mind should be employed in observing and analyzing itself. A mind observation during meditation or any other time shouldn't be limited to only a neutral observation of thought stream. In order to undoubtedly crush identification with the mind and see that the mind takes place in me, rather then I am this formation – the mind, one must look deeper and more closely into the mind's dynamics. One must see that thoughts and emotions arise in emptiness and dissolve in it. A thinking process always takes place using the ordinary, learnt and even cliché pathways. In this regard it is not possible to speak about any expression of the mind's independent will and choice. Most importantly, one must notice that it is not possible to draw a line between the thinking mind and the "external" world, including the body. Both of these play out a continuous interaction showing that they are different expressions of a single phenomenon.

Yet, the most crucial aspect of awakening is a deep and sincere striving to recognize as well as fearlessness and readiness to refuse this person. If one presents these powerful symptoms, it is not long before awakening will take place.

Enjoying this Relative World

Although I use words like *an illusion* and *a dream* when I talk about this ordinary world, it doesn't mean it is something one should abandon as worthless or isolate from. The amazing abundance and beauty of this expression of the Absolute is unquestionable. What makes existence here miserable is strongly believing to be an individual human being. After having seen I am that in which this magnificent expression takes place, the existence in this world can bring so much joy. However, even before seeing fully one's true nature, one can shape their own perception in a way that makes their life much lighter and more harmonious.

All is Well with This World

The informational field of modern society is overloaded with news and emotions full with discontent and indignation that unwittingly create a notion that nothing is right with this world and it gets only worse. It is a narrative that builds up in the mind of an individual unnoticeably, roots itself deeply and is constantly maintained. Anger and the feeling of injustice are often almost a default reaction to all those appearances that in some way don't correspond to the idea of how things should be. As a result of the speed and effectiveness of the flow of information it is easy for such a heavy perception of the world to overtake many minds.

However, it is not an objective notion properly characterizing this reality. First of all, there is no single objective reality that each of us simply experiences slightly differently. There is only one Consciousness that plays in itself a whole world through each of its individualized expression, i.e. each mind. Because the Consciousness is one, playing it all in itself, strong similarities can be found among these worlds. Second of all, we mix up our direct experience with its interpretation, or we take as a reality that which is only secondary – attitudes, ideas about right and wrong. Thus, we take an interpretation of the mind as an objective reality and cannot distinguish anymore what it is that we truly experience and what is only an interpretation of this experience.

Thirdly, all is an expression of a single Consciousness or the Absolute that plays out in itself countless scenarios. And it plays out in itself not only experiences, events, but also attitudes towards them. Therefore, any notions created in the human mind about ethical, unethical, beautiful and ugly are never objective. In any case they cannot be the absolute truth even if most of the other minds agree on that. They have only a relative meaning within the world of the mind.

The abovementioned, however, doesn't mean that one should take up an extremely passive position and conformist attitude in everyday matters or events on the society scale. It means to see all in a greater perspective, to see that everything is an expression of the single Consciousness and my deepest being is identical to that. Also all processes and events of this relative world are real in their own context; yet, they do not possess absolute truth. This understanding allows seeing everything without a tragic connotation and with true compassion.

Who's Right and Who's Wrong?

When I was following discussions about some current societal processes, I was surprised to realize that each participant's words, although sometimes opposed to opinions of others, seem true. I read an opinion of one discussion participant about some issue and concluded to myself that he is being very reasonable. Then I was reading further the viewpoint of some other discussion member that completely rebutted the previous opinion revealing other aspects of the matter, and concluded that I was wrong, the truth is on this side. The discussion continued, and some third participant also expressed his stand on the issue showing the shortcomings of both previous statements. And again, I couldn't agree more. Yet, after re-reading the discussion one more time, none of the opinions seemed wrong, even though they opposed each other.

Initially I concluded that all of these people are simply smarter than me as all that was said seemed correct and I couldn't see a fault in any of that. However, by facing similar situations again and again in which I learnt different, sometimes radically different, opinions regarding some worldly issues, I realized that everyone is right. Looking from each person's perspective, the particular individual's opinion becomes completely understandable, and indeed it has its own relative truth. However, on an absolute level nobody's standpoint reflects the truth fully. All opinions arising from a personified viewpoint are subjective. And it couldn't be any other way. They have their truth only within each individual reality.

This understanding creates a great relief. It calms down the mind because it turns out it is not possible to reach a complete agreement in many complex and important issues of our time anyway. And thus, there is no need to fight for the victory of one "correct" opinion and certainly no need to try to persuade others about the correctness of one's own standpoint thinking that the others simply haven't understood yet what you already know. It turns out the world is not full with fools. Each mind is a unique individual reality that cannot be more objective than the worlds of other minds while this world is seen through the prism of a person. This understanding not only frees from the burning need to prove others one's own truth, but also from judgement and anger arising from not being able to accept different opinions.

However, an idea that every intelligent person must have its own opinion on the relevant political, societal or cultural matters is being cultivated. And it is assumed that non-existence of one clear, definite opinion indicates a lack of education or a low mental capacity. Thus, this narrative promotes the creation of a limited mind and a desire to defend a narrow angle.

Understanding this, an inner discomfort no longer arises in situations where it is appropriate to express a personal viewpoint, take a position; yet, one doesn't have such a desire and feels that nothing of value could be said in the context. The consequence of this, obviously, is a risk to become boring in the eyes of others. It doesn't mean, however, that it is not possible to actually enjoy experiencing the exchange of views as in a good theater, or sometimes out of fun due to some impulse or enjoyment of communication express a narrow opinion and take part in discussions. After all, an opinion that arises from a person and is not categorical can remain and actually does remain because until this individualized form exists, also its tendencies and characteristics continue their expression.

It is, however, important to understand that this openness to all kinds of viewpoints does not mean indifference or a nihilistic attitude towards all worldly expressions. This openness and the recognition of the relative truth of others' opinions create infinite compassion and love. No space is left for judgement and anger. It is seeing the situation from a beyond-personal stand and sympathizing with every character of this game knowing the source of them all.

To Understand Each Other

Awakening to one's true nature unavoidably brings changes in relationships with others. Although I see there are no "others", everything keeps manifesting in a way as if there were. The "others" turn to me as if to a person awaiting my reaction as from an individual. Of course the ordinary dual game is very familiar; yet, not always there is an urge to participate in it. Furthermore, it becomes increasingly more difficult to understand what is the reaction expected. By itself this liberation from the common, socially accepted reactions in no way should be perceived as undesirable. It is a natural expression of awakening. Yet, to others it may not always be understandable. The lack of reaction or a different reaction instead of expected one can create misunderstandings.

Sometimes I perceive situations inadequately, or rather, the way I perceive them does not correspond to the way others see it. Sometimes people understand what I've said quite differently than it was intended. For instance, what I see as a completely neutral situation or neutrally spoken, others sometimes see as blaming or a judgmental statement. Often people read emotions from my facial expression that are absent internally. It surprises me each time – does my face or voice truly express some attitude that is non-existent in my experience, or am I a mirror to others in which their expectations, subconscious voices or inner anticipations are reflected?

An inability to react in accordance with socially accepted norms can create an impression of a lack of empathy or indifference to others. However, it is merely an impression based on a customary perspective from a personalized worldview. By knowing oneself as the ever-present Consciousness, all experiences in this reality are permeated by compassion and love toward all beings. Compassion arises toward any kind of suffering irrespective of their seeming cause as the only source of suffering is not knowing oneself. If we define empathy as an ability to feel what the other feels using imagination and to suffer along, perhaps to some extent this ability actually does decrease. When I see others suffering, what I feel is true compassion and love toward them; however, not because I admit that a seeming reason for their unhappiness is truly an unfortunate event, but because they don't see what they are, they believe they are a person and thus suffer.

After awakening I certainly don't feel indifferent; yet, I understand there is nothing wrong with what is happening, nor there is any injustice. It is clear that the Absolute expresses itself in that form in that particular way, without a reason. What is even more important – I realized that also my and others' feelings toward them (feeling sorry for them, helplessness and even anger) are also a manifestation of the same Absolute; therefore, making it all a spectacle played out in one Consciousness.

Due to these differences in the perception, communication with friends and family can become troublesome at times, thus possibly creating some complications in the relationships. However, after awakening I actually enjoy hanging out with friends much more than during the uneasy period right before when I often felt I don't want to see them. There are some friends that have alienated; however, it has been always their choice. And I still don't know if there were any exact reason for that, but it doesn't matter anyway.

Altogether, these misunderstandings are a complete trifle in comparison to indescribable happiness and freedom that comes by knowing oneself as the beyond-personal. Great freedom and lightness is brought into relationships after awakening. Feelings like jealousy, distrust and tendency for being controlling or attempts to change some aspects of the partner are simply non-existent after recognizing one's true being.

Stress, the Unpleasant Part of This Reality

The underlying cause for stress is fear. And this fear arises from experiences that makes one believe that one is an autonomous, vulnerable person acting in this world, which is full of competition, conflicts and very little love. Such a perspective that I am a person whose life completely depends on my own actions, and this physical person is all that I am, can indeed generate great fear and a belief that this life is a battle field.

It is not of course the fault of the person that it sees this reality in such a way. The reason for this person having to live in such a reality is not because it is doing something wrong, worries about non-essentials or is overly sensitive. Such an experience and a person that lives through it simultaneously arise in the Consciousness, without having any causal link between them. A person is not an independent being that could make decisions about specific experiences it will go through.

While the Consciousness is experiencing everything through an individualized form in its particular expression, it is exposed to all kinds of relationships and events of this reality as well as negative impacts arising from them. The character is exposed to stress while the dream goes on.

However, when one's true nature has been recognized, all is increasingly observed as from aside. It is similar to watching an action movie while sitting on a comfortable sofa in safety. Although sometimes the stress and tension reflected on the screen overwhelm the viewer, largely it is not experienced in such amplitude as the character in the movie does. Whatever happens, the viewer's awareness of being in a complete safety and knowing that all displayed is only an actor's play is always present to some extent.

By knowing oneself as the Consciousness, the common component of this reality – stress – cannot penetrate one's deepest being. It can create waves on the surface only. Still, sometimes unpleasant experiences can take place; however, at moments of higher clarity it seems funny that such irrelevant, impermanent non-essentials can have any impact at all. Everything is observed from the position of absolute peace, which, however, can sometimes be invisible to others because the particular role must play out what needs to be played out, also agitation and unease if that is the case. Yet, there is no relevance to how others see it; although highly stoic position in situations that seem highly stressful in the eyes of others can create an impression of inadequacy or indifference.

Nevertheless, if awakening to one's true nature hasn't taken place yet, it still is possible to consciously decrease inner anxiety created by stress, thus making one's existence more pleasant. The practice of meditation and self-inquiry without a doubt promotes more conscious thought stream and slowing down of mind's movements; therefore, it is a valuable daily ritual. The contemplation of death, traditionally practiced by Buddhists, which is to be aware of the impermanent nature of the objective world, shows a calming effect by reducing fear for one's survival. By knowing with absolute certainty that this physical body and this person will sooner or later cease their existence, everyday worries lose their significance. Being aware of the fact that it won't be possible to keep any possessions or personal gains, such as reputation, for very long in this reality, and that in fact everything has been lost already, provides a feeling of great freedom and inner peace.

There are more sensitive people who start reading a book by reading the end of it first because knowing the outcome, they can perceive all events of the story more calmly and not get overly attached to the characters of the story if they must die, thus making one's reading experience more pleasant. The end of our story we know already, even without any specific interest. Thus, we can use it in our advantage by shaping our current perception of the reality.

The Cult of Busyness

Most of the people nowadays are overwhelmed by busyness and hurry. The relentless stress created because of it suppresses the joy of life and leads to physical and mental health problems. Still, people are proud of their busyness as if it was some achievement or proof of one's distinct value and indispensability. And others find it a respectable property as well and, therefore, further encourage this destructive notion.

People let themselves be pulled into countless tasks that overtake almost their entire waking life. They work hard, hurry to make money for some imagined future moment when finally one will be able to get a rest and enjoy life. Most commonly such time never arrives. However, if one does actually succeed in creating some savings, then either the individual is not anymore capable of recognizing that moment of enough and stop because he/she has turned into an "eternal worker" who isn't capable of functioning in any other way, or one's physical and mental condition has been impacted by long-term stress to such an extent that a permanent grumpiness and background of suffering have been established. And this in turn, makes one experience their existence as if through a gray, bleak fog.

To put oneself in such a state has never been an active choice, however. It is a result of learnt beliefs and notions about this world. Since childhood we have been taught that "one must become competitive in order to succeed, make a career without which a successful, honorable life is impossible." The idea that working hard is respectable and that it is the only way to create a "successful" life and achieve "a lot", whatever that means, is deeply embedded in our subconscious mind. It is fear that forces us rushing forward because otherwise "I won't be loved," says our subconscious mind.

Nevertheless, at the same time there is a different kind of busyness that is not at all lead by ideas and fear embedded in the subconscious mind. It is not hard to imagine representatives of some certain professions or active people that aren't acting only for the sake of acting. These are vocations that are based on a true passion and a natural pull to act on some cause, for instance, in order to promote an excellence in one's field of activity, to solve some issue, thus reducing the suffering in this world. Busyness like that is not founded on fear and ego's efforts to create an illusion of its significance. Yet, these are rather exemptions than a norm because most likely no one that has gone through the traditional system of education has remained unaffected by these destructive notions.

Of course one can say that for many such busyness is simply a fight for survival because otherwise it would not be possible to earn enough to cover all the needs. However, it can relate only to a little paid work in combination with specific life conditions that has created significant unavoidable expenses. However, also in cases like that a conscious or unconscious notion about hard work as a ground for successful life most likely prevails. And such an understanding undoubtedly projects each individual's experienced reality accordingly. An idea that one must be hard working for life to be successful is truly sad. Moreover, also the understanding about what is a "successful life" consists of mostly learnt, alien ideas. This belief limits expressions of life that could be lighter, more joyful; yet, they aren't because deeply in one's subconscious mind such a possibility is not even considered.

Many of us can't truly stop for a moment and do nothing. Not "do nothing" – watch television, sink into countless stimuli of the internet or read books, but truly be in the current moment absolutely socially useless and unproductive. Instantly a learnt feeling of guilt of not doing anything creeps in. It is not a virtue to be constantly bustling if this bustling is a result of deep, hidden fear. It is suffering and unawareness. In fact, it is similar to a slavery in which an individual doesn't realize its condition and all its activities are led by a hidden conviction "if I am not good enough, I won't be loved."

Of course life scenarios play out as they must. And it is not possible to avoid what the particular facet of Consciousness must experience because who is there that could avoid? However, those who start to be aware of all those beliefs that are not created by one's own experience, but are accepted as truth in an early childhood without questioning them, can consciously promote filtering out such false beliefs from one's individual reality, thus making one's existence much more pleasant.

The Lost Present

Many people these days seem to have lost the ability to truly live. They live for an image of themselves, which is a stabilized understanding of themselves as a sum of characteristics, status in society and physical properties. They worry what this person or an imagined "I" should achieve, what should be done next. True enjoyment of peace and existence hardly ever occurs. It is hard for many to stop and experience the moment exactly as it is without any added interpreting and assessing thoughts. Many have constant fear whether this imagined self will turn out to be successful, and, therefore, design their own life's story as if a rating of life's achievements will take place in the end of the life followed by a reward or condemnation if nothing of value has been gained. However, by shaping one's story like that the present is lost. The mind unceasingly reviews what has been done in the past or plans future steps. Yet, all we have is the present.

At the same time sadness without any particular reason, prolonged depression and inner agitation are quite common phenomena for modern people. And it is undoubtedly related to certain conditions of this relative, perceivable world – an enormous amount and speed of information, rather unnatural lifestyle and environment for our species as well as the current socioeconomic system.

In recent years mindfulness has become rather popular as a concept that promises solving at least some of the issues mentioned above. Mindfulness is to experience all perceivable clearly, without the cloudiness of thoughts. It is to see ordinary appearances from a fresh and completely accepting viewpoint. A regular practice and enhancement of such a perspective undoubtedly bring results and make one's existence more light and joyful. However, often in organized meditation classes a revelation of deeper understanding that would answer to the most essential question of all - what is it that lives or what experiences life - is not promoted. Nevertheless, even without delving deeper into the exploration of the self, these "more superficial" practices are of a great value as a phase along the way. Yet, in order to approach recognizing one's true nature a step further must be taken by releasing the thought "I who practices mindfulness".

The mind of an individual is the same as the world that is individually experienced. The Consciousness gains experience through the prism of a limited perception by expressing as the mind, which is the same as the person, an individual or a human being. When that is seen, all is experienced each moment as an absolute perfection.

What to Do in This Life

Since an early age we have been taught that the success of life is measured by outwardly visible life accomplishments. It is customary that in the funeral as the achievements of the deceased its career successes and children raised are mentioned. All of that is embedded in our subconscious mind making us since young age perceive the value of life and self only in the perspective of outward expressions. It is taught that to be in a present without any purposeful activities that are oriented toward the future is simply a waste of time because the highest aim is to be useful and respected in society. No value is seen in the life of a human about whom the only thing that can be said is that he/she simply was.

Outwardly visible achievements are an imagined measure for evaluating life. By recognizing that we have inherited such a system of values without ever questioning it as if it was absolute, we can finally liberate ourselves from the excess weight created by this notion and the common background of self-accusations that accompanies our existence.

No being, no experience and no moment are less valuable than others. And it is not simply a humanistic, romantic attitude. Looking from the perspective of the Absolute, it truly is so. It is only the mind that has created any kind of comparing, evaluating belief system. Of course such a statement might seem self-understandable; however, it is not at all easy, first of all, to recognize the great impact this deeply embedded belief has on our perception in our daily life and, second of all, to liberate ourselves from it.

Nothing has to be done or has to be achieved in this life. There is nothing to prove to anyone and no need to justify one's existence. If, however, something happens to be done that is valued as respectable in society, it is not an achievement of the person. It happened so without a reason, simply because the Consciousness expressed itself through the particular role in such a way. Inaction or boredom possesses similar importance or unimportance.

Nevertheless, what must be done, must be done. Even if someone decided to be completely passive from now on, thinking that no activity has a great significance anyway, unavoidably some circumstances, thoughts and desires will arise that will promote some action. The mind itself is an activity; therefore, while it moves even a seeming inaction is an action. Thus, what can liberate us, is not merely changing our outward expressions, but rather cleansing the mind of the redundant, inherited beliefs that inhibits us from a true relaxation even for a moment, and forces us to be in a state of constant light anxiety and urgency.

Releasing Expectations

Expectations poison our experiences. They take us away from the now into an imagined future. Furthermore, they create a feeling of imperfection and lack preventing us from truly enjoying the moment whatever it may be. To live with a constant background of expectations, which often can be left unnoticed, means to frequently experience disappointment and bitterness. Higher education and a greater access to information create preconditions for the mind to have higher expectations, which then, in turn, lead to greater dissatisfaction and bitterness because experiences don't correspond to the imagined ideal.

The world is seen as wonderful and complete again when it is experienced without expectations. Looking at everything from the beyond-personal viewpoint, it happens naturally. However, it is possible also for highly educated minds to liberate from expectations by consciously transforming one's perception. A valuable practice is to get oneself into a situation or go to a place that is known to be quite unpleasant and which normally one would try to avoid from. Being there stand for a moment, take a few deep and slow breaths, relax the mind and look at all surrounding as an interesting phenomenon, as if seeing it for the first time, without any judgment and let it be. All of it is played out in the Consciousness, and all of it is complete in every detail. Such a practice can be introduced as a habit consciously changing one's perception each time when even slightest resistance to what is happening is felt or a desire appears for things to be different.

A resistance to what is happening causes suffering. This applies also to the physical pain. When the pain arises, the first reaction of the mind is to resist and repulse. However, if at that moment we don't push it away, rather consciously focus our attention fully on the experience of the pain, accepting and merging with it, it no longer causes suffering. This approach, however, could have its limitation when it comes to a chronic pain or in cases when in parallel to experiencing pain one must carry out other activities that require attention.

A distinct personal desire to change the world indicates toward great suffering because such a desire arises out of seeing this reality as faulty. It doesn't mean though, that one can't take part in activities for the greater good with intention to reduce the suffering in the world knowing that "my role is a tiny part of this grand theater that is complete in itself" and not getting attached to the fruits of this work.

The Relevance of Personal Growth

Word combinations like *personal development* or *personal growth* are often used in various spiritual growth teachings and seminars. Also self-improvement methods, which are based in understandings of the modern psychology, use these terms extensively. If an aim is to improve one's circumstances in this life as an individual, then consciously shaping the image of oneself in this world understandably is useful and even unavoidable. However, making a connection between personal growth and spiritual development is not straightforward.

By assuming that what is meant by a phrase *spiritual development* is a more or less conscious process to approach awakening, personal growth seems like an opposite to that. The person itself and its exaggerated relevance are the main obstacles toward the irreversible recognition of one's true being. Furthermore, looking from the absolute perspective, no growth is possible to that what we truly are, as it is eternally perfect and permanent. And to wake up means to recognize self as that. Accordingly, the word *growth* has a meaning only within this relative world. And no changes that occur to dream characters impact the higher reality.

Such personal improvements like the reduction of the lack of self-confidence and fear, the increase of acceptance of the different and compassion are auspicious and positive in this relative world of course. Not only they make life more pleasant for an individual, but they also seemingly create better preconditions for spiritual awakening processes by clearing away disturbing thoughts and destructive emotions. Apparently this reality expresses in a way that seeming changes in experiences, perceptions and characteristics of an individual take place, which sometimes have positive effect on approaching the recognition of one's true self. However, this cause and effect relation is real only for the dream characters that are played out in the Absolute. And these positively perceivable changes in a human are rather a symptom indicating approaching awakening not the cause for it.

Nevertheless, regardless of how these activities towards the improvement of one's own personality are perceived - as crucial for awakening or as merely a side activity until the recognition of one's true nature takes pace-, it is unavoidable if an inner desire or necessity to change some expression of oneself exists. An active release of accumulated misleading and suffering causing notions, beliefs and suppressed emotions of the individualized consciousness before awakening is a widespread scenario that is being played out in this dream. This release, however, to a large extent happens by itself without a conscious effort of an individual. Furthermore, it keeps appearing all the rest of the life while the body exists after one's true nature has been recognized.

The ambiguity of the cultivation of personal growth hides in the fact that a risk exists to grow an attachment to this "polished" personality, newly created identity, which again is nothing more than an idea one has believed in. It is of course a more beautiful and attractive idea, however, in no way it gets one closer to self-recognition. Thus, a potential trap is created, which is an increase of ego or a strengthening of an idea of the individual "I". It is often called a *spiritual ego* by referring to people who have accumulated quite abundant knowledge on the intellectual level, have had many experiences in different practices, have long been working on getting one's personality closer to the imaginary spiritual character, however, haven't recognized their true nature. And, therefore, a new, powerful idea of "I" has been created, which now has a tendency towards arrogance and exaggeration of one's significance.

However, also the creation of the spiritual ego is a game played out within the Consciousness itself; therefore, looking from the absolute perspective, it cannot be perceived as a mistake. This statement, however, should not be viewed as an excuse for the above mentioned adverse tendencies because as long as one believes in the reality of their own person and its autonomy, one will feel responsibility and consequences of their actions and thoughts.

A Person Cannot Truly Love Itself

We often hear that among various advice for life and for self-improvement a necessity to love oneself is mentioned. However, first of all, it is not possible if we are talking about a person that must love itself. Moreover, one cannot fall in love with anything simply using will power. One can consciously have a look at a particular object in a way that can promote one seeing its beauty and uniqueness; yet, true falling in love is not a person's decision.

Secondly, *loving oneself* is often mistaken for emphasizing the superiority of one's personality or physical body over others or attributing some highly rated characteristics to the image of oneself. And it has nothing to do with love. It is merely an expression of ego or believing in one's importance and realness. And it is also a reason why people with a purer consciousness find something unnatural and wrong in this idea of loving oneself. Simply, it has no relation to true love, and these people sense that.

The only thing that is capable of loving (and which actually is love itself) is our deepest, truest being – the eternal, ever-present Consciousness. And it always is unconditional because there simply is no other "type" of love. It of course doesn't have to actively love anything because it is its natural state. A human being cannot love anything; yet, love can be experienced through it. Thus, the mind cannot influence it in any way – does the falling in love with someone takes place or not.

While one's true nature is not seen permanently, human beings usually don't feel love toward themselves as individuals with all their characteristics. I didn't like my person as well. I thought I am suffering from it when I didn't see yet what I am. Now I see it as infinitely dear and innocent. And it is not because the personality itself would have changed. It is perfect in its imperfection - an expression of the Absolute that cannot be faulty. Of course this reaches out much further then one's person. I love everything so much that it almost makes me cry. And it is not the person that loves. Outwardly it appears so because the expression takes place through this form, which is only a façade.

Nevertheless, how to be in a greater harmony with oneself while awakening hasn't taken place yet? It is possible to shape such a perception of the reality that makes all experiences more pleasant. It is losing the idea of self-importance, not perceiving life and oneself overly seriously, reducing expectations as well as understanding that perfection is only an idea in the mind that has no real basis. Cultivation of mindfulness daily is a great tool to reduce the judgmental and analyzing thoughts and to see the beauty and absolute completeness in everything, also in one's person and its expressions.

Meditation and Self-inquiry

An intellectual understanding doesn't stand even close to true experience. An understanding on the level of a mind on topics like how this reality functions and what is a human being, does possess value. However, alone by itself this intellectual understanding cannot help in recognizing one's true, immortal nature. Thus, an important part of the self-recognition process is meditation and self-inquiry.

What is meditation? Various notions exist about it, most of them having a similar main understanding about it as a practice for slowing down the mind and increasing awareness. Differences among various notions are defined by different goals of meditation. Often guided meditations offered at yoga studios or self-improvement seminars are led by rather worldly goals. They can be a relaxation, quieting mind in order to reduce stress, to gain inner peace, which will then help reaching more balanced mind and emotional condition in life. Another prevailing worldly aim of meditation is the increase of mindfulness, which is to see all surrounding clearly, without an interpretation, here and now. Mindfulness is to not give a name and assessment for any experience that arise in our perception, rather enjoy it directly and fully by accepting all that comes and letting go of all that must desert.

The practice of mindfulness is very popular in Western world these days as it truly has some remarkable practical gains for leading one's life more pleasantly. They are the discarding of habitual thinking routes, patterns and perception frameworks, thus creating an opportunity for the creation of a fresh and unaffected perspective, which in turn fosters better circumstances for creativity and innovations. Moreover during the state of mindfulness the mind is clear, concerns about the future and repeated remembering and living through the past events cease as there is only this moment that is absolutely perfect in itself. That in turn reduces stress and increases productivity and a balance in any activity.

Although these worldly gains are worthwhile by themselves, and I certainly do not wish to diminish them, they should rather be called side-effects of meditation not the deepest aim of it. Each of course can have their own aim and none of them are wrong; yet, if we use the word *meditation* referring to that which has been derived from Eastern cultures, then previously mentioned meditation goals are rather superficial in comparison to what potentially this practice can offer. **The main goal of meditation is enlightenment**. Meditation is a conscious tool for decreasing movements of the mind in order to recognize what I actually am. The aim is to see that my deepest being is not the mind, which becomes clear when the magnetizing movements of all perceivable on this screen of perception are reduced and thus one's true nature behind all accepted beliefs, accumulated notions and ideas of "I" is recognized.

Meditation is often equated to concentration. However, it is not really concentration because it is the mind that can concentrate; yet, the aim of the meditation is to see the mind as though from aside in order to stop identifying with it and to recognize one's true being. Nevertheless, initially for it to be possible to "get" to this "behind the mind" space some concentration is needed, especially at the beginning of the meditation practice when thoughts are quite chaotic and it seems it is impossible to silence the mind. Then an effort is needed; however, only until a certain degree. And by no means should one ever be hostile to oneself, as that would only create frustration and even more movements of the mind. The effort must be gentle, so that it doesn't create discomfort, yet, persistent at the same time. Actually, the only effort that must be applied is related to bringing oneself back to the position of the observer when an absorption into the thought stream has happened again. And this bringing back to awareness is gentle and neutral, without any judgment towards oneself or feelings of powerlessness.

Meditation is a balance between concentration and relaxation. At its base it is relaxation; however, certain effort must be applied not to sink into unawareness – no to fall asleep or to forget the now into the thought stream. Initially it is not easy to find this point of balance and stay in it for more than a few seconds after it has been found. Yet, in time, as it is with any new activity, by practicing regularly this point is reached, and it becomes possible to remain in it increasingly longer. When certain maturity has been reached in the meditation practice, the effort must be applied less and less; it could rather be called vigilance then. Whereas the relaxation of the mind can reach such a degree that the fear of temporarily forgetting one's identity of this reality and giving up one's collection of notions disappears.

In order to realize the highest aim of meditation, it is worth combining meditation with self-inquiry, in which the thinking mind itself is used purposefully by observing and analyzing one's experience from a fresh perspective thus ridding oneself of learnt notions. Within this approach the mind is not observed from a neutral position of the observer, rather the mind asks questions to itself. However, no "prepared", conceptual answers are given to these inquiries. To find an answer the mind assesses and observes its direct experience looking from the position of absolute mindfulness that is free from learnt, accepted notions and beliefs. In such a way it gradually cleanses itself from an accumulation of false beliefs until finally that which experiences everything, including the mind itself, is recognized.

Progress in Meditation

The essence of meditation is not difficult to grasp. And initially, while only reading about it, it might seem that it shouldn't be too difficult. Yet, by practicing it one faces various obstacles and odd experiences. If one practices meditation regularly, it could be of value to know at least about the most significant effects expected, what they indicate of as well as approaches to ease these difficulties.

The positive impact of breathing techniques or *pranayama* on quieting the mind is well-known. Breathing methods or simply an observation of breath before meditation can bring a significant support in reducing mind's movements. At the beginning of the meditation practice when it may seem the mind has gone completely out of control, it could be a potentially helpful method. Hatha yoga teaches precise breathing techniques that encompass a prolongation and deepening of inhale and exhale, which in turn have a direct impact on the heart-rate and on slowing down the mind's activity. However, also simply observing and slowing down breath provides a great help in relaxing the mind. By applying this, one should exercise moderation and not be violent towards oneself of course. Conscious breathing can be of use not only before meditation, but also during it if the mind has become overly active and it is no longer possible to not get absorbed by the thought stream. In such a case the mind can be put in use by employing it in concentration on the breath in order to relax the waves of the mind.

Often in relation to meditation people speak about stopping the mind and mind control. However, in a way that it is usually understood, the mind and thoughts cannot be stopped; therefore, there is no need to try and do that as that would only create frustration due to repeated failure. It is so because it is the mind itself that could be trying to stop the mind. To that what I am, there is no need to stop it. All that is necessary is to recognize that my deepest being is not this mind. When that has been seen, then, first of all, the mind actually slowly becomes more submissive and calm, and, second of all, for me as the Consciousness there is no need to forcefully stop or change anything.

At the beginning phase of the meditation practice quite a rapid increase of mind, thought aggression often can be observed. First thought that usually appears in practitioner's mind is that one is doing something wrong and that regression has taken place. Yet, it is not so. Quite contrary, it points to the effectiveness of the practice that has been done so far, and one should continue the same way.

Why does then after a successful meditation the rebelliousness of the mind increases? First, I must mention that this increase of the mind's noisiness is only a relative observation because by slowly improving ability to observe the mind from the position of peace, finally one comes to see how chaotic and hasty the stream of thoughts has been.

Secondly, one can observe also a phenomenon of an actual sudden increase of mind's uncontrollability, which has now replaced a usually moderate thought stream with an incoherent, hasty and even aggressive line of visualizations and memories. There can be two reasons for this. It can be the resistance of the mind as a habit to the process of consciousness's focus change from the perceivable, worldly impressions to that which perceives everything, the source of perception. The second reason can be that along with the processes of spiritual awakening the disintegration of all accumulated notions, beliefs and suppressed emotions takes place. And during this disintegration process the particular accumulated imprint (a belief or an emotion) can be brought into the light to be released. The process is not pleasant, and it can raise doubts on effectiveness of meditation. However, it is a temporary, possibly even unavoidable, phase. Certainly it is an auspicious sign.

When a certain level of maturity has been reached in meditation, one can experience another quite common phenomenon – a fear appearing in the instant when meditator starts to lose the awareness of the perceivable world, objects, and the feeling of "I" as a person after having successfully stayed in a position of the observer for a longer moment. Most often at this point the practitioner returns back to its ordinary state, in identification with the mind. Some people report that having found themselves in a complete darkness, nothingness, they got scared of this vast emptiness in which there wasn't peace promised, feared of possibility to go mad and thus returned back to the usual perception, this reality. This fear is the mind itself because it is a step into the unknown, into the behind-mind reality. This is a threshold that can be crossed by being willing to let go of the individualized "I", personality and by having courage to wake up. This fear is understandable of course because at this moment the mind in fact must surrender. It must let go of its position as a leader. And in order to surrender one must long strong enough for "home" or for the recognition of one's true nature as well as have trust.

This fear during meditation can be spontaneous and intense. Therefore, it is easier to overcome this threshold gradually, each time taking a small step forward while slowly getting used to the new perception and gaining confidence that forgetting and momentary disappearing of one's person by no means indicate the end of existence and in no way it impacts my true being. The unpleasant and empty darkness that is experienced by some practitioners is not the reality that will be experienced after crossing this beyond-mind threshold. It is the projection of mind's fear imagining how the existence could look like if the ordinary reality disappeared. This projection of course couldn't be further from the truth. By recognizing that also this "black nothingness" is just the mind, the unpleasant experience disappears.

Sometimes during meditation one can observe sudden flashes of bright light. They can be momentary or sometimes can last a bit longer. That is an excellent sign as well. Some call it the light of Consciousness. If the moment of flash lasts longer, the mind can get scared from this as well and rush back into the ordinary state of perception. Also in this case it is possible to surrender and recognize oneself as that bright light or return back again to the ordinary, limited state of consciousness.

Overcoming Thoughts Require Determination

When I started the meditation practice many years ago, the beginning wasn't easy at all. Thoughts seemed completely wild. I switched between two main positions – forgetting myself in thoughts about something (some past event or future plans) or being in a process of falling asleep, when abstract and chaotic images are starting to replace thoughts. During that time it seemed impossible to sense that moment of silence between the thoughts. Also it wasn't clear to me how to observe the mind because my whole perception was completely occupied by the mind and thoughts themselves. It was impossible to take a single step back to see it as from aside. With my eyes closed I couldn't stay in a conscious state for more than half a minute as immediately sleep would overtook me.

There are people who succeed quite quickly in having their thought stream slow down and in gaining the ability to observe the mind, or at least they claim so. However, most commonly it takes quite some time after the beginning of the meditation practice until results become detectable. It can be even a year of a regular practice. And it requires quite firm determination because when it comes to meditation it's easy to give in to procrastination because the benefits are not immediate and progress can be almost unnoticeable.

Most commonly the beginning is rather slow also because it is not clear yet what must be achieved simply because one hasn't had that kind of experience yet. Theoretical descriptions are not enough to get such a precise notion that would immediately help understand what is the state desired. Yet, when one has succeeded to sense that unchanging, deep peace lying behind the thought stream, behind the mind for at least a moment, this feeling is "recorded" in one's consciousness, and next time it is much easier to tune into that state.

The fact that one day after months or even years of practice one will gain the ability to impede the thought stream is not a sufficient consolation for someone who doesn't feel progress yet and suffers from an overactive and chaotic mind of course. In cases like that it would be of value to devote a few minutes several times a day for observation of thoughts, not even calling it a meditation. Observe the dynamics of thoughts, how they arise out of nowhere and disappear into nothingness. Such a short period of time won't require too much effort as well as won't bring too great disappointment if one doesn't succeed.

At the same time it is useful to implement a habit of neutral observation of one's own mind, thoughts and all surrounding at times when one is waiting for something, for instance, in a line to see a doctor, or when one must engage in an activity that doesn't require intellectual involvement. Thereby, gradually the ability to observe one's mind, thus slowing down the thought stream, will be developed. It is important not to try and forcefully stop the thoughts because it is not possible to do it directly with the help of will power anyway.

Internal Dialogue Maintains This Dream Reality

Internal dialogue is such an ordinary phenomenon that it mostly stays unnoticed. However, it accompanies almost all of our waking hours, except for the moments when attention is fully occupied by some external stimuli such as watching a movie, reading a book or observing some intense event. As don Juan taught Carlos Castaneda, stopping internal dialogue opens the door to start *seeing*. Continuous internal dialogue in combination with wandering thoughts maintains this dream reality when there are little or no external stimuli. Internal dialogue maintains the movement of the mind, which in turn makes the dream to continue. The moment they cease, identification with the particular person or the role starts to dissolve revealing the totality of everything.

Yet, this dream is "installed" in a way that before the particular facet of the Consciousness has experienced what must be experienced, there is a powerful resistance for the dream or this reality to be interrupted even for an instant. Each night in the deep sleep phase such an interruption takes place; however, it doesn't happen consciously, and after it the usual reality always resumes because not everything that the particular individualized consciousness must experience has been exhausted.

Internal dialogue is not an unequivocally negative phenomenon, though. Often it is a way how to find a solution or shape an intellectual understanding of some issue within oneself as well as to calm down or inspire oneself. However, in order to be able to successfully practice meditation or mindfulness and to recognize one's true nature in the end, the stopping of internal dialogue is of critical matter. As it becomes especially active at moments when strong external stimuli are absent, the simplest way to trick the mind so that the inner voice and the thought stream would cease, is to consciously let one's attention be fully absorbed by some perceivable sensation as if it was rich and intense experience. For me the most effective seems to be merging attention into surrounding sounds without distinguishing them individually, without interpreting or analyzing what is being experienced. However, also looking at an abundant landscape, at flowing waters of the river, at waves of the sea, at flame movements of the fire or at swinging of the tree canopy in the wind can undoubtedly bring the desired result.

At the moment when attention has been fully absorbed by the particular phenomenon, it is important to simultaneously retain awareness of the silenced "inner" space of the mind. It is a truly enjoyable moment, a deep relaxation. Gradually the activity of the mind will return; however, in the course of time the length of the moment of silence will increase. In such a way it is possible to train the ability to interrupt internal dialogue and thoughts almost instantaneously. And this in turn is a truly valuable skill when it comes to practicing meditation, self-enquiry or mindfulness.

Movements of the Mind

Why is it that at the moment when all duties have been fulfilled and finally peace could set in, one could sit doing nothing just enjoying the present, the mind desperately seeks for any reason to keep itself busy? The mind is a movement. If movement ceases, also the mind no longer exists. Only the pure Being remains. And this mind, which can be called also a cluster of tendencies or a program, a scenario that must be played out, shows great resistance to be stopped. When movements naturally cease and there is no reason for activities, immediately new excuses are found or imagined to interrupt the moment of silence. The belief that "one shouldn't just sit doing nothing" is deeply embedded in our minds. Such beliefs arise from the full identification with the individual "I"; and activities take place just for the sake of being active without any far reaching aim.

Often we see someone living in relatively excellent life conditions. Everything is rather peaceful, and life unfolds without too many complications. Outwardly it may even seem quite an enviable life. However, even then the particular individual always finds some problems, worries and purposefully looks for something to be concerned about, something undesirable, even when all is fine. Not always these activities of the mind are directed towards negative emotions, though. It can express itself also in different kinds of busyness, like countless projects and hobbies. The reason for keeping oneself busy is never explored because it seems self-understandable that it is simply auspicious to be always active, it is welcome and it actually maintains this life. The last reason is actually true, if by life we mean this "dream" that is maintained and created by activities of the mind.

During the process of awakening for some period of time a pull towards two opposite directions can be observed. One is a desire for peace, for being present. And the other is the mind's desperate effort to create a movement in order to maintain its existence. Such a place can be quite horrible, and can make one feel as if trapped in a corner.

When I experienced such a state, I refused any activities that were suggested by the mind, seeing it as a trick of the mind to plunge back into various tasks in order to delay the recognition of my true nature. However, at the same time I couldn't be in the Now, in full awareness as the mind wouldn't cease to create new and new reasons for starting the thinking process or things to attend. Thoughts like "Perhaps I should read a book or, better yet, clean those bathroom tiles for once" were frequent visitors. It's called procrastination before awakening. Although I knew where attention should be placed, an extraordinary pull to drift the attention towards the objects of the "outside" world was experienced. Previously such absorption into external stimuli created satisfaction of having filled the day with various activities; yet, during the process of awakening it created the feeling of unpleasant emptiness and meaninglessness. However, it is most certainly an auspicious state because no turning back is possible at that point. There is no longer an option to forget oneself in the ordinary life. The only way out is to recognize that within whom all this is being played out.

Experiential Meditation for Unraveling the Illusion of Space and Separation

This type of meditation could be called also *a self-inquiry*, which is an observation and evaluation of one's experience from a fresh viewpoint by trying to get rid of learnt concepts. In comparison to a common understanding about meditation as a method for quieting the mind, this approach purposefully uses the thinking mind itself.

Sit down comfortably so that the body is at peace. Close your eyes and observe your breath for a brief moment. Inhale deeply, exhale slowly. At this moment all that we truly know is our current experience. The rest are assumptions, notions and thoughts. Focus attention on hearing. Hear surrounding sounds. Then pay attention to where does this hearing take place. At which moment does an intangible conviction arise that this hearing indicates of some kind of an object that creates sounds and is located at a certain distance from you? Observe this experience - where does hearing take place?

It takes place here, always here. It never takes place somewhere outside, as we don't have any direct experience about that. We don't have any experience about the "outside". Try separating this hearing experience from thoughts and visualizations of the possible source of the sounds. Only hearing is. And try to look again where does it take place. Observe how habitual it is for us to assume without checking that it takes place somewhere outside, in some external world, although our direct experience shows the opposite. Hearing takes place in you. We have no proof of sounds that spread in the space out of one point reaching our perceptual organs. All we can be truly sure is hearing, and it takes place here.

By observing purely only hearing, your direct experience, a conceptual imposition or an illusion that there is some kind of a source of the sound, which is located at a certain distance from you, is lost. It always takes place here. Can you define where exactly is "here"? Can you imagine at all the existence of "somewhere else"? At the moment you think about it, it is already "here", at the center. Where ends "here" and starts "there"? There are two possible options – either all that can be experienced is always here or you are everywhere.

Now focus your attention on the bodily sensations. Keep your eyes closed and feel the lightly vibrating sensation that we assume to be our body. Now focus on some particular point of this vibrating cloud. Focus on the point that usually is interpreted as the foot that is touching some surface. And with eyes closed try to release this sensing from the thoughts, imagination of the body or surrounding objects. Release it from any assumptions for what each vibrating sensation might mean. Focus only on your current direct experience. What can be said about this cloud of vibrating sensations that we usually call our body? Where does this sensing take place? How far from you is it located? Is it a meter, half a meter or a few centimeters away? We cannot tell it because all sensations arise and fade away only here. Observe that anything we pay attention to regardless of whether they are sensations pointing to our palms or knees always takes place here. It is not located in any distance from you. It is an experience that always takes place here.

Now open your eyes. Out of all types of perception seeing is the one that creates the strongest illusion of space and separation. Pay attention to some point that is located, as it seems, the farthest away from you. Observe what is it that you truly experience now? Do you experience some real material object located some distance away from you? Or is it only seeing, and at this moment you don't know anything more about this object then only this seeing? Release any associations, thoughts about what it is, what kind it is, how far it is located. All that you truly experience now is only the seeing. Now observe where does this seeing take place? Does it take place somewhere over there in 5 or 3 meters distance where the seeming object is located, or have you just believed in it? When we rid ourselves of learnt notions, it becomes clear that seeing always takes place here, it never is somewhere outside. It takes place in you. It is never somewhere there at a place where the object of seeing is seemingly located. The locality is mind's interpretation. Observe this.

All experiences show up and disappear. They are impermanent. However, we don't disappear in the flow of these changing experiences and impressions. We can see their impermanence while having a stable sense of "I". Therefore, in order to spot this impermanence as impermanence, the observer must remain unchanged. What are you? All you can experience (seeing, sensing, hearing, smelling and tasting) is here. We don't even have any direct experience about existence of space, about existence of any object. What is that permanent being within which the flow of experiences takes place then? What is it that is aware of these experiences and thoughts?

The Absolute Wakes up from [Your Name]

- Where do you point to when you say "I"? Don't give an answer that you think is correct. Base your answer on how you feel now and what your actual experience shows you.

- *"I" is this human being, a person.*

- Let's have a look at this person together. What does it consist of? Can you name elements of which this person consists?

- *The physical body, characteristics of the personality, my thoughts and memories...*

- What is its core element from which all else arise? What does your experience so far tell about it?

- *The physical body.*

- Let's have a look more closely at each of these elements that seemingly make up this person.

   Your name. What is it? It was attributed to you by your parents. It is simply a sound with its writing. If you no longer have this title, is there less of you? No.

   Your characteristics and abilities. Have your characteristics always been the same since the birth, or have they changed – some more, some less? They are changeful. Yet, what is it that can observe this changefulness? Isn't it so that there must be some ever-constant reference point in contrast to which it is possible to spot and to evaluate such a change of characteristics at all? Imagine you return back to your childhood at some particular time. And remember that feeling of "I am", the feeling of your deepest being, that point from which you observed everything when you were a child. Now compare it to how it is now. Has this core feeling of "I am" changed?

If we take away from you some of your characteristics or we change your profession, in your opinion, does it alter your deepest being, or does it only impact your expressions? Anyhow, there is not less of you, and also that core "I am" feeling doesn't change, does it?

Your memories. Your life's story is included in this category as well because it has no existence anywhere else apart from your memories. Forget everything for a moment - everything that has ever happened to you, any ideas about your personality. Is there less of you now? Has that core "I" feeling changed or become weaker? It can be a bit scary to imagine losing memories; however, after releasing them for at least a moment it becomes evident that you are neither your memories, neither what has happened to you.

Your thoughts. As it was with memories, by giving up also thoughts for a moment it becomes clear that I remain even without them. Furthermore, they are extremely fickle. If you were your thoughts, you would be chaotic and uncontrollable, without any chance to focus on something for more than a few seconds.

Your body. Can you be aware of the processes that take place in your body each second, how incomprehensibly complicated they are? Are you truly this body, or are you simply experiencing it? If your core being really was this physical body, then you should be able to regulate or at least be completely aware of what happens with you – all complex biochemical reactions, cell division processes, etc. However, we know about it as of some kind of external object, external phenomenon. And you say it yourself – "my body", "my head" and "my leg", not "I - body", "I - head". And if you had to lose some part of your body, does it make your core being smaller? The external expression would become different; yet, nothing of your deeper "I" would be lost.

You experience all those elements; yet, they are not you. Who are you?

— *I don't know. Although I rationally understand that I cannot be all those things, still identification with this person doesn't leave me.*

- It is because there is a strong habit not to look deeper, but associate only with this idea about you. It is understandable of course because it has been taught and cultivated all your life since the birth. Yet, it is only an idea because you can consciously rid of it for a moment remaining intact at the same time. Try to sense what stands behind all these ideas and what it is that experiences all of this, meanwhile always remaining unaffected.

- *It is hard for me to sense anything other.*

- This looking/sensing is different than we usually would do. Mind cannot do it. It would be like making a ray of light illuminate its own source. In an ordinary way it is not possible. One cannot see itself directly. It is, however, possible to be aware of one's source, of one's true nature by not turning to it directly, but by "taking a step back" or "zooming – out". What are you?

- ...

- You don't have to provide any name or label to it. Mind will desperately try to fit it into conceptual frames of reason and give it a name; however, then it is not going to be IT anymore. Keep on asking yourself these questions and carry out such self-inquiry. Gradually the ordinary way of self-perception will be weakened, and self-recognition will take place.

Self-observation for Distinguishing the Pure Being from the Conceptual World

Focus on your direct experience. Have a look at everything from a completely fresh perspective, without any concepts, ideas about how things are.

Hearing

Close your eyes for a moment. What is it that you experience now when you hear surrounding sounds? Liberate your mind from thoughts and any associations. All your attention is directed only towards hearing. Hearing is. Now spot that moment when your direct experience is imposed with layers of thoughts, when you switch automatically from direct experience to unproven assumptions, beliefs. Now, for instance, your direct experience is hearing. This experience of hearing is changeful. It's all you know. However, at the moment when a thought, a conviction arises that you hear the barking of a dog or the sounds created by the neighbor mowing a lawn, it is no longer your direct experience. It is an interpretation. This is the moment when one goes from being mindful into living in a conceptual world, in the mind. Bring back your attention to hearing. Is there any evidence on the dog that barks or the neighbor that mows a lawn if you experience the hearing purely as it is, without any thoughts on top of it?

It would be complicated to operate in this reality if one was in such a perceptive state all the time. It would be like being an infant who hasn't yet developed any conceptual notions, any ideas about this world. However, such a conscious looking and analyses of this reality allows us to see the unbreakable connection between the mind and this reality as well as to see that my person, idea of "I" is part of the perceivable reality, not my core being.

Seeing

Open your eyes and carry out a similar investigation with seeing as was in the case of hearing. Look at some point in front of you and distinguish your direct experience at the current moment from the thoughts about an object that is being seen. Notice that instant when a direct experience – the seeing – is imposed with the mind's created interpretation. Notice how quickly and unwittingly that happens. This habit is so deeply rooted that we no longer distinguish where our true experience ends and where the interpretation of the subjective mind starts. Unnoticeably we take this conceptual interpretation as an objective reality.

Observe the seeing itself. Does this direct experience of seeing deliver true experience on the visible object itself? Can one really say that this seeing brings proof for the independent existence of a particular object? All we truly know now is this seeing. Everything else – ideas, thoughts about the object, about its seeming distance from us, its outlook, functions and any associations, memories that are brought up in relation to it – are mind's impositions, not the objective experience of this moment.

Seeing in comparison to other ways of perception such as touch, tasting, hearing and bodily senses, makes one believe in the physical separation of "I" from the "external world" most strongly. However, if we liberate our minds from believing that this is how this reality is, that this is what our experience indicates of, then it is possible to see that spatiality is merely a construction of the mind. Yet, it is hard to grasp it for the mind because this understanding reaches beyond its framework of rationality.

Touch and bodily sensations

Any kind of perception always takes place here. Similar to hearing and seeing, also touch and bodily sensations take place here, in the non-local center. Close your eyes and direct your attention to that cloud of lightly vibrating sensations that you usually assume to be your physical body. Liberate this experience of sensing from any mind's impositions – any thoughts about what each sensation means, what they seemingly indicate of, any evaluations. Only sensing is. Does this pure sensing is irrefutable proof of the existence of your body? Only when thoughts appear about what each sensation could mean, an idea about the body arises. Therefore, it is merely a mind's construction.

By carrying out an in-depth investigation into each of these types of perception it becomes clear that none of them provide a direct experience of the surrounding objects, spatiality as well as autonomous objective existence of one's own body. Thus, we have no proof that these exist, or, in other words, the mind cannot be separated from the "external" world. This reality is the mind in its broadest meaning (not only thoughts, inner convictions, but also emotions and all types of perception). And although each individualized consciousness lives its own reality, i.e. its own mind, it is not possible to draw a strict line between these many minds because consciousness that experiences through them is one.

Techniques for Quieting and Observing the Mind

As mentioned in an earlier chapter, the primary practice for gaining at least a glimpse of one's true nature is to observe the mind in a way that reveals its coreless-ness and thus allows seizing identification with it.

This section provides a few rather simple techniques that can be applied during meditation or any other time of the day if one faces difficulties to quiet the mind. Not all of them will be equally effective for everyone; therefore, a bit of experimentation is needed to find what works for you best.

In meditation

These techniques are merely for calming down the waves of mind; thus, they are needed only until more clarity has been gained. You may find that sometimes it is enough to apply one or two of them for a few minutes only before meditation. Sometimes the only way to not give into the wanderings of the mind is to continuously practice some of these all throughout the meditation session.

- Consciously observe the breath and bodily sensations that appear due to breathing. Practice abdominal breathing. Breathe through nose slowly and deeply.

- Consciously breathe as in the previous point with a brief holding of breath between an inhale and exhale and between an exhale and inhale.
- Apply mantra (any word in mother tongue that is relaxing and tuneful enough) – initially consciously chant it in your thoughts, then let go of any effort, let it flow and transform as it wants (faster, slower, louder or quieter), and hear it in the background without any effort. Do not think of its meaning if it has any, simply hear it.
- Focus attention solely on the surrounding sounds without analyzing and interpreting them. Hear all of them without focusing on one source only and merge with them fully. This will stop internal dialogue quite effectively.

At any time of a day

If one is sincere about recognizing one's true self, the conscious perspective change shouldn't be limited only to a meditation session once a day or less. The striving to wake up should permeate any time of the day, and thus several approaches can be incorporated during other daily activities or brief pauses in between them.

- Several times a day devote a few minutes to observe your thoughts, their dynamics – how they appear out of emptiness and vanish without leaving a trace. By simply observing them you will create a habit to perceive your mind as from aside.
- Be consciously aware of everything that is taking place during any activity that doesn't require great intellectual input. Be mindful without any mind's commentary or evaluation, thus, training a neutral attitude towards all that's happening.
- Practice spotting any evaluating, judging thought in the instant it arises - be aware that it appeared, recognize it as an old habit and release it. After a while you will be able to catch it before it expresses itself fully, and in the end such thoughts will stop arising altogether.
- When the mind is particularly anxious and there is a pressing need to calm it down, isolate yourself from all outer stimuli (either physically

or mentally) and observe your breath making it slow and deep. As simplistic it may sound, it is an effective method because breath is related to the activity of the mind.

Selection of the Best Q&A's

This section of the book provides some of the best questions that were asked and answered either on Quora.com or my blog nothingeverhappened.org. They pose some intricacies on relevant matters, and perhaps can provide an added value to the readers.

Are we responsible for everything that happens in our life or is everything decided by fate?

Often we wholeheartedly wish for something. Some of us even use certain *law of attraction* techniques to make sure these thoughts realize. However, more often than not it doesn't materialize. For a while we feel discouraged. Then we forget.

Yet, after a while the situation has changed, we find out things about ourselves or the world that we didn't know before and are supremely happy that what we wished for before did not happen. Therefore, we don't even know what is the most auspicious scenario for us…

Fundamentally this is a question about free will. The person and its life story is the dreamed, not the dreamer. This can be quite easily tested by looking where do one's own thoughts arise. If one believes that he/she is an independent person deciding all the matters of their life, then it should be the one that generates their own thoughts, which are at the base of our decisions. However, upon closer inspection we can see that we experience thoughts, we don't construct them. They appear in our mind already formed. Same applies to our emotions.

And the thinking process is based on concepts, ideas and beliefs that are not directly generated by us. They have either arrived already formed or they are a result of experience (that we didn't knowingly generate). This is so subtle that it is usually unnoticeable.

However, an idea of a human is impossible without the concept of free will. The mind simply cannot accept such an idea because at the very base of its own construct of the world is the idea about an independent, autonomous human being that one identifies with.

Yet, when the Consciousness awakes from the temporary delusion that it is a human being, it sees that a human indeed has been only an idea that one has temporary believed in.

What is the reason for existence of the Consciousness? Why does it purposefully hide from itself?

The only thing that can be said about the reason for existence of the Consciousness is that it is the only way how the Absolute can experience itself. One could say that it is how the Absolute plays out within itself countless scenarios of expression. Why is it necessary? There is no answer to that; similarly there is no answer to question "What is the meaning of life?" It is the human mind that gives rise to questions like these because it perceives this reality from a dual perspective trying to look for and finding causes and consequences. On the absolute level of truth questions like these don't arise simply because such concepts don't exist outside of the reality created within the human mind. It would be as non-sense as asking a question like "How does the time smell?"

The Consciousness "allows" itself to be seemingly separated in countless beings and forgets itself so that this cosmic theater could take place. Otherwise no relationships, various experiences and no friction among different facets of the Consciousness would be possible. Of course such an answer is not completely satisfying to the human mind because, still, it is not understandable why so much suffering is needed. Why would the Absolute need that? The answer is that apparently there is some kind of enjoyment in all that is being experienced. However, it must be viewed from a wider perspective understanding that within this dream there is no one, united, objective reality. Each mind is a whole separate world.

Along with the evolution of an individualized consciousness (evolution apparently being an integral part of this reality) the feeling of separation becomes increasingly unbearable. This leads to a proportional increase of suffering among all experiences and decline of the pleasure created by this dual reality. Accordingly, an individualized consciousness, which is at a relatively lower level of evolution, is not interested in and doesn't have any questions about the purpose of this existence and why should there be so much suffering in this world. It mostly enjoys existence in its particular form. And what it fears the most is the loss of its individualized existence.

Therefore, those to whom such questions arise, already experience conscious or unconscious longing for the "re-union" with the Absolute or home. Everything that is not love causes them to experience suffering. One could say that the process of awakening for these kinds of individualized facets of the Consciousness has begun.

Is it possible to have such a great identification with the person that awakening is impossible regardless of a long, conscious path and practice?

It is not possible of course to predict when exactly awakening will take place (during this lifetime or not). However, the fact alone that for years true interest has been expressed and practices and other activities have been consciously carried out with an aim to recognize one's true nature indicate that on some level awakening processes already take place. If they didn't, there wouldn't be this deep and sincere interest at all. Therefore, it is only a matter of time. Awakening doesn't take place yet because something within the particular individualized seeing has not been exhausted - too strong tendencies, too great interest in experiencing worldly adventures still remain, no matter in what area of life.

The only thing that can be done is to let play out what must be played out more quickly. This reality apparently expresses itself in such a way that an individualized consciousness remains within identification as a person until this person has experienced this reality to such an extent, so diversely that after reaching a certain degree, gradually an enthusiasm toward realizing oneself as an individual as well as interest into enjoying this world through the narrow prism of a person are lost.

Are all ideas of enlightenment a barrier to enlightenment itself?

I am not sure if I had been here where I am without conceptualizing about enlightenment and a path towards it at first. I would not have known were to look for. Sure, ideas can never be IT; yet, they serve for providing directions. Because I had established an intellectual understanding comprehensive enough to know what I should do and because I felt the truth is there, I was exceedingly determined.

In my experience an intellectual understanding, at least for westerners, is quite important for further awakening processes and direct experiences to take place. Also for me it was a crucial part of all the self-recognition process.

Nevertheless, they can get in the way if they are too misleading. And in the end all ideas must be abolished to see the truth. Yet, on the way they can be a useful tool.

Can awakening occur suddenly, as shown by Eckhart Tolle's example, or is it impossible until gradual ridding of illusions has taken place?

Although sudden awakening is not my experience, many stories of awakening have illustrated that it can manifest itself twofold - gradually by slowly ridding of false identification with the persona and accumulated beliefs or suddenly. Eckhart Tolle's awakening is indeed a well-known example of a sudden, extreme shift in the consciousness. This story, however, has a continuation. After awakening he spent a few years in quite an inadequate condition for this reality, i.e. "spent two years sitting on a park bench."

In accordance with my seeing, an individualized consciousness needs time for integration of the "new" seeing. And this integration, as we see, can happen before awakening, partly before and partly after or after, as Eckhart Tolle's example shows. In a case when integration has not yet happened, or it has happened minimally before seeing the truth, the moment of the perspective change is radical and can cause a complete collapse of the previous understanding of the world. This can make the mind unable to function within this reality for a while. Then, as we see, time is needed for the individualized form, the mind to adapt and regain its ability to take part in this game in accordance with its rules. However, this time in a self-aware state.

It's very likely each awakening is sudden in a way; however, often this irreversible instant of self-recognition is not experienced as extremely radical because before that a gradual integration to the non-personal perspective has taken place. Also a significant release of accumulated mental and emotional buildup has taken place. Thus, an impression of graduality is created.

Can one become spiritually enlightened from being physically in the presence of a spiritually enlightened being?

The power of transmission shouldn't be undervalued. We all know we influence each other unknowingly, just by presence. And what a power it is to meet someone who represents exactly what one strives for so deeply! Will it trigger self-recognition on the spot? Perhaps, if one has reached the ripeness needed. Perhaps not yet, but it certainly will leave traces.

I experienced that meeting and even talking to an awakened being greatly promoted inner awakening processes. I don't even remember what he said, and it didn't matter the slightest. I experienced several glimpses of seeing the truth while being in proximity to him; however, they didn't last. Yet, I knew that something had irreversibly shifted in me. Then, after half a year or so the interruptions in seeing the truth ceased completely. And this seeing continues to grow clearer and deeper ever since.

That being said, still, it all happened within a dream. The awakened being was met because awakening was already taking place for this individualized consciousness, and the dream simply reflected it by playing out circumstances and situations to make sense of what was happening. Similarly when one is asleep and there is some noise in the room not loud enough to wake up, yet audible, the noise is translated into some situation within the dream, so that it makes sense.

So, the answer is - yes and no.

Do enlightened persons seek other enlightened persons as their partner or do they prefer non enlightened persons as their partner?

The question is based on a misunderstanding that after awakening one is the same person as previously, only now it has gained some new attribute, new seeing. However, the perspective changes completely. One recognizes that it is not a person, and there are no other persons as well.

Furthermore, there is no active seeking for a life partner because to seek means to suffer from incompleteness, which is not the case for enlightened one. One lets the dream manifest itself as it must, and sometimes it happens so that one individualized expression meets another individualized expression and enjoys experiencing this dream together. There is no resistance to what comes and goes.

And it also doesn't matter if that other is awakened or not as there is no active "selection" taking place based on some criteria. All is seen as the Consciousness playing out as many forms, equally lovable.

How can one walk a spiritual path and desire money at the same time?

Look at it differently. See the need for earning an income as a necessity for a fair exchange. That's true - we rarely can afford not to get involved in the socioeconomic system of this reality. That is just how this dream is constructed. Our dream bodies need food, shelter and care. While we express ourselves through these forms, we have to play by the rules (more or less).

See money for what it really is - a convenient mean for evaluation and exchange of resources. Nothing else. And it's great to do something that is of value for others in return being able to receive different kind of value that one can't produce (shelter, electricity, food, etc.). That seems quite a fair exchange.

If you remove the unpleasant association of money as a tool for gaining power, for accumulation of resources, then there is absolutely nothing wrong with it. And in the absolute sense there is nothing wrong with this dream either. Our attitudes and feelings about things within this dream are part of the dream.

Why have I become emotionless after spiritual awakening?

Integration must be taken into account as it takes place before and/or after awakening. During that period all kinds of changes in expression can take place. One can become overly emotional, crying out of the intensity of love towards everything or for the time being become emotionless perhaps because of the deep enjoyment of the all-pervading peace and, therefore, being temporarily switched off from this reality. These things can fluctuate. Emotions are an appearance as everything else that can be perceived. Yet, you remain as the ever permanent Consciousness, and that's all that matters.

Once someone has achieved enlightenment and ended the rebirth circle, where does he/she go?

Enlightenment is to recognize that I am the ever-pervading, everlasting Consciousness, which had temporarily forgotten itself in an individualized form. Therefore, after one's true nature has been recognized, it becomes clear that there is no he/she that has to go somewhere. There never was. I see that this person, which I am playing out now, is merely a wave in the ocean – temporary, without its own independent existence, without its own substance, just a role that has to be played out. This form will play itself out, and then it will no longer be. If some tendencies remain that still need to be played out after the cessation of this "physical" body, perhaps a new dream character will arise that will fulfill those remaining tendencies/projections. Yet, the Consciousness always remains as the Consciousness.

This question implies that there is some ongoing evolution within the Absolute. Yet, time is only a by-product of the mind. I see that what I am is always permanent, beyond time and space limitations. I see that time is experienced within me. Outside of this relative world the word *time* is an empty sound, without a meaning because it truly doesn't exist. Although I am still limited in this particular angle of perspective, I see that I am this ever present unchanging screen or the Consciousness in which all the relative worlds are played out. I have no idea what else will be played out/experienced here.

Out of all forms of beings are humans the only ones that possess a strong pull towards self-destruction? And if so, why?

Suicide is perhaps an extreme example; however, almost everyone experiences daily activities and impulses of self-sabotage.

Although obviously I do not have a direct experience of how other forms of beings (animals and plants) feel, it's very likely they do not possess such tendency because they don't have the thinking/analytical mind. Although they are not aware of what they are, that is, they are not enlightened, they haven't created an idea of themselves as individuals; therefore, they are always here and now. The thinking mind is the one that constantly creates concepts, believes in them and as a result creates a whole world, which then it mistakes for a reality and suffers being "locked" in its narrowness.

The tendency towards self-destruction points to an unconscious desire for purity and truth. As we know in our deepest being that our personhood and all matters related to it are only mind constructs or a temporary role, then at certain moments a pull towards destroying it appears in order to get closer to the truth. No one strives to be unhappy even if outwardly it looks as if someone purposefully acts to achieve that. Presumably it is an unconscious behavior to get rid of and destroy something that is not authentic or has become unpleasant. Such behavior, however, doesn't really get one closer to the truth because destroyed dream appearances and objects doesn't affect the state of consciousness - whether it is awake or asleep. It is more like a symptom of an inner striving to free oneself of that which doesn't bring peace and love.

For quite a long time before recognizing what I am I did not want to be. Not just physically. I wanted to cease existence fully because all I knew about myself was clearly fake and, therefore, unpleasant. Because I knew what I must do in order to reveal the truth (thanks to the directions of awakened beings), I did not let it be an unconscious and destructive process. Outward expressions of destruction were limited to a moderate social isolation and ridding of materialistic values as well as memorabilia that would remind about the past and the life's story of the person.

Why is the state of enlightenment so hard to describe?

Behind every word there is a concept. When we hear a certain word our mind instantly brings up associations that normally would help us understand quicker and operate better in this world. However, they do not help when we want to talk about something beyond this world, beyond comprehension of the mind. These associations generalize and distort trying to reduce the awake "state" to the level of this dream world so that the mind can conceptualize and understand. The language of this dream world is simply not designed for talking about what is outside of this dream.

When I speak about the "state" of enlightenment, I feel regardless of what kind of words I choose I can never pinpoint it. I can improve the description by becoming more skillful at choosing words like writers and poets do. Yet, it is never going to be IT. There simply are no words for illustrating that level of subtlety. And if a word is created for that, in time it accumulates other associations becoming quite like many other words – overused and overgrown with associations.

What are examples of "promises broken" upon spiritual awakening?

The only promises that can be broken upon spiritual awakening are those of the mind. Surely, there are plenty of conscious or unconscious expectations tied to awakening. And these expectations come from the concepts and ideas of awakening, which are far-off from true awakening. They are merely ideas of the mind, a part of the dream from which we are waking up.

Apart from the mind's expectations no promises have ever been given regarding spiritual awakening. Who is there to give such promises? There is no one. The Consciousness is waking up from a dream in which it temporarily forgot its true being and adopted a narrow perspective of an individual being.

What are then examples of **promises of the mind** that are broken upon spiritual awakening? The heaviest one is that after awakening the seeker will become an awakened person. Obviously, that one must be broken because awakening is to recognize that I am not a person, the person has been merely an empty facade or a role in this dream.

Another quite a common belief is that the life from outside for the awakened one will dramatically change. For instance, one won't ever have to work again, one will suddenly possess such a great radiation of love that everyone will instantly notice it and regard them as a Teacher. Life will certainly completely change; however, not necessarily from the outside. Knowing what I am and what all else is, dramatically changed my perception of all I encounter, that is, how I see everything. It can result in changes of life's external matters, but not necessarily. Some visible changes will probably take place; however, they can be rather small, hardly noticeable to others. Yet, the awakened being doesn't care for appearances like that at all.

The expectation - everyone noticing one's radiation - arises from the mind's desire to strengthen one's significance. And this is a desire that fuels the dream to go on. This must be abandoned or surrendered before awakening along with the idea of an individualized or autonomous "I".

In conclusion, awakening is sudden and gradual at the same time. Many expectations are related to sudden changes in outer appearance of one's life. However, as it appears awakening never stops, and the clarity of the seeing keeps on growing while this individualized form remains.

Is there a spectrum of spiritual awakening?

After an instant recognition of one's true nature, accumulated beliefs and notions that have been accepted without questioning and have been reinforced for years slowly fade away unveiling the truth more and more clearly.

As it seems the deepening and an increase of clarity of the seeing never stops, at least while in this form. There is no testimony on what happens after the cessation of this form, though (whether some kind of individualized expressions keep taking place or not).

So, we can see that the spectrum exists. We can observe it ourselves by looking at how our own individual clarity and expansion of awareness increase in time.

Yet, our fundamental being is always as it is - ever-lasting, ever-present and absolutely permanent. And to spiritually wake up is to recognize it as one's true nature. Thus, we are already absolutely perfect at our deepest being. The spectrum of spiritual awakening only indicates the degree of one's clarity in seeing the true nature of all existing.

Why after meditation does my drive to do work in this world decrease?

Quite naturally as the mind and thought stream due to meditation have slowed down, an active expression of an individualized I or ego decreases. And that translates into disinterest in worldly activities because the mind IS the world you experience.

Before I recognized my true nature, for 2 to 3 years I had completely lost interest in this world. All I wanted was truth, and I saw it cannot be found somewhere "outside". Therefore, I didn't want to socialize, attend any cultural, educational or entertainment events. If I had to, it brought a sense of meaninglessness and falseness of this reality. I couldn't understand what others find so joyful and interesting about this "theater". I just wanted to quit the game. I went to work only to earn for the living. Fortunately, my workplace of that time wasn't too demanding.

Now, seeing everything from a very different place, I find enjoyment in all kinds of experiences. I do not have an extensive interest in the matters of this world, but I no longer strive to isolate myself from all that. I am involved in worldly matters doing different work now, and I allow things to happen as they must. I enjoy what this person must do without the heavy burden of identifying with this role.

Can one operate freely from their true self with intense shame continuing to lurk around?

It's not that all remnants of past tendencies disappear right at the moment one recognizes their true self. They keep lingering around for a while. Because of inertia, old thought patterns and feelings still show up, but they gradually lose their power. After a while one notices, "It's been a long time since I last felt like this or that."

When I woke up to see what I am, I still experienced lack of confidence, shyness, but it didn't matter anymore at all. Previously I would suffer because of these aspects of my personality. Now, I don't mind at all. It's absolutely OK that this person plays out in such a way. It's perfect as it is; I no longer see something needs to be fixed. That being said, these qualities are slowly fading away. It's almost unnoticeable, but if I compare how I feel now and how I felt a year ago, I see the difference is significant.

I am sure it is the same with feelings of shame. The more deep-rooted they are, more time it will take for them to fade away. Yet, they will because they are not being fed anymore as you have come to see your true nature.

How do I be open minded & non - judgmental?

I used to practice following approach. Whenever I noticed judgmental feelings and thoughts arising in me, I imagined what could have happened to the particular person making him/her act like that. For instance, if I interact with someone who is impolite and rude to me without any apparent reason, I imagine in my mind perhaps the person is in physical or mental pain for some specific reason (specifics help), therefore, currently isn't able to be friendly with the world. Surely the cause might be very different; however, the exact reason is irrelevant.

When someone is highly self-indulgent, I think to myself that he/she is simply brought up like that. Perhaps he/she was the only child in family or one of many children causing him/her to fight for attention among their siblings, and he/she is just yet not aware of this, without any bad intention. Judgment is replaced with an understanding.

Now, whenever I hear about someone committing serious crimes like murder, rape, I instantly understand that the particular person is locked in its own horrible reality. Probably he/she has experienced a lot of violence towards him/herself during childhood, probably has never felt loved, probably has lived in a degrading environment. Seeing this, judgment and anger are automatically replaced with compassion.

After a while this practice stops being a practice, and acceptance, compassion becomes a natural reaction in all cases.

Is it normal to feel fear during meditation?

Every time I meditate I feel surrounded by evil and horrifying beings. It feels like they are closing in on me and I have to break the session off. It feels like something out of a horror film and it happens every single time. Could I be "inviting" spirits while meditating? I know this sounds nuts.

Fear during meditation is quite a common phenomenon. First, I want to say this is a sign showing that you're progressing in your meditation practice, which is great. Therefore, it would be the worst advice to suggest stopping it. It is common for a practitioner to face the resistance of its own mind during meditation. In a way the mind is like a habit that resists to the focus change of your consciousness that meditation brings. It is a focus change from an ordinary attention toward outside objects, thoughts and feelings to the new focus toward the source of that which perceives everything. To stop you from going there the mind will project the fear, which is stored in your sub-consciousness.

This should be viewed as a certain test that must be overcome. That is, one must be willing to face those "demons" and "evil beings" that mind has projected, without fighting or resisting. One must be courageous enough and thirsty enough for truth to be willing to take the position of surrender holding an attitude that I am willing to let go of my individual "I" to see the truth, or if I must die in order to find what I am, I am OK with that. Obviously, the practitioner won't die or be harmed, but the mind will surely be extremely convincing that exactly this will happen. One might not be able to overcome this with the first try, and that's completely understandable. Thus, it can be done taking small steps, every time going a bit further, and seeing nothing bad really happens. Eventually the fear will be exposed as false and will fade away.

Why does life feel fake after I meditate?

This is a wonderful sign. It means you are coming to see that this world is a construct of the mind. Before this you believed undoubtedly that you are a separate person living in and interacting with an objective world. And now the meditation practice has started to reveal the true nature of this existence. Therefore, you have the feeling of life to be fake and that it's not fully real, which is true.

If this perception bothers you and you feel this somewhat robs you of fully enjoying all worldly experiences, know that it is temporary, at least based on my experience. For quite a while I had a feeling that between me and all experiences, objects there was an invisible wall. I had a feeling I couldn't fully and deeply experience any object because when I tried to completely merge my attention with it, I was left with a sense that it is empty and unreal. I just couldn't find its core, which is absolutely correct as no object has its own independent existence. The answer was not to be found somewhere outside.

I came to understand that the source of all things in the world, including me, a human being, was the one that experiences everything, the one that cannot be seen because it is THAT which sees everything.

Now I see all objects and experiences take place in me (which is not the person, the person is another experience). And I do not see this life as fake like before, and I can fully enjoy it. I just know what its reality is and where it comes from.

How do you meditate on the Supreme?

I used to meditate on the Supreme. Until I realized there is only the Supreme. Now when I am meditating, I simply rest in my Being – infinitely peaceful, unshakable and happy.

At the time when I still felt separated, in meditation I was practicing seeing through all things that I am not or, to be more precise, all things that are not my true being. Everything I can perceive, I am not. This process of gradual removal of the false identities and beliefs revealed that which experiences everything, the Supreme.

Which type of meditation suits you? Why?

When I am alone, I am sitting quietly, sinking into my true being and letting all movements of the mind, experiences and thoughts, slowly fade away. Then I am everything and nothing, beyond time and absolutely content.

When I am with other people, on the street or in the bus, I look at surroundings, not interpreting anything. I love everything and see it all takes place in me. I notice the contrast between the constant change of everything that can be perceived and the absolutely unchanging point or space in which and out of which I am experiencing it all.

There is no particular reason for the exact way I meditate. I guess, this is just how it has evolved and what is most natural for me.

What is your conception of God?

There is no longer any concept between "I" and God. It is all that is, or only God is. It brings laughter thinking about how I've been looking for the ultimate truth or God in an objective world when actually all this seeking was played out within itself, the one to be found.

If I become more "awakened", will I lose my personality and become a pointless blob of nothingness and lameness?

No, you will only come to realize what you have always been. And it certainly isn't a pointless blob of nothingness and lameness. You won't even lose your personality. You'll just finally be able to see it is only a changing decoration or a role in this theater. And you'll experience this role and theater being played out in you and as you, never affecting that which you really are, the Formless.

While the dream goes on, this form, the body and personality, exists, regardless of the fact that you have come to awake within a dream. Then finally one can love this personality, this innocent body and not try to change it because one sees the absolute perfection in everything.

Meditation and mindfulness are requiring detaching and non-attachment. Can one remain focused on life goals adopting a "letting go" or "let it be" attitude?

Certainly. Adopting a "letting go" or "let it be" attitude helps clearing away an emotional cluster around all life matters. Often this emotional cluster involving feelings like "If I fail, I will be unlovable" makes our vision blurry and actions too desperate or premature. When one sees things clearly without the cloudiness created by subconscious beliefs or personal identification with a current matter, the focus on things that must be done will certainly be even more distinct.

However, I must add, the goals themselves might change after gaining more clear perspective on everything.

What are some practical ways to observe one's thoughts without judgement?

To neutrally observe thoughts during daily activities outside of a meditative state certainly is a greater challenge than doing it while in a conscious contemplation. After a while the thought stream observation during meditation will naturally bring its effects also into other life segments like awake and dream state.

However, what one can do during everyday life is to repeatedly remind oneself of the nature of this reality. Remind yourself that this is a grand spectacle played out in the Consciousness and that I (the Consciousness, seemingly limited in a certain perspective) am simply experiencing a role or this person, which must be played out, including its thoughts that might not always be positive. This understanding will quieten the judgmental voice within us. In the course of time, combined with meditation practice, this should lead to a genuine seeing of what one's true nature is, leaving no judgment towards the thoughts of this small person.

What helped me were subtle reminders that I would encounter with during daily activities, like PC desktop background that states a short powerful phrase of what reality is or images of certain teachers whose gazes through the pictures instantly remind me of what their core messages are. Here are some examples of the reminder phrases:

- Nothing happens and could ever happen to you. Your essence, the Consciousness, is invulnerable.
- This world is a grand theater. People are merely roles that are being played out by one actor, the ever-present, ever-lasting Consciousness.
- You are already free and immortal. This person with its physical appearance is merely your temporary form, nothing more than a costume.
- You cannot be anything that is changeful because you are able to notice any kind of change only because your true being is beyond time and space.

What role do parents play in shaping their children's perception of life so that their perspective wouldn't be contaminated with delusory notions and misconceptions?

Parents undoubtedly have a major role in shaping their children's perception of the world. However, it is not a coincidence that the particular individualized consciousness expresses itself in its specific form in this specific world, this socioeconomic, cultural environment. That which reincarnates and enters this world with a specific form is a cluster of beliefs, strongest characteristics and tendencies that must be played out and experienced. They "enter" in specific circumstances that allow it to happen.

Children are not born like blank sheets of paper. Initially at a very early age while no conceptual understanding about this reality has been formed and while the analytical mind, therefore, is not active yet, actions are based on instincts. Then, as it often is in the case of animals, it may seem for us that the child is enlightened and sees clearly all as it is. In a way this seeing is closer to enlightenment then that of most adults because it is a state of complete mindfulness. In such a state everything is still being experienced directly and without mind's interpretations in contrast to majority of adults who mostly live in their own conceptual minds. However, it cannot be regarded as an awakened "state" because although an identification with a person has not been established yet, they (small children and animals) are not aware that they are the ever-present, eternal Consciousness.

Along with the formation of ideas about oneself and this world at some point, sooner or later, children start to express a certain perspective that cannot be created only due to existing environment. Often, however, the particular individualized consciousness finds itself in life circumstances that as if reinforces and revives those tendencies that have been reincarnated in order to be liberated. Therefore, although a direct correlation might be visible between a tendency of perception of the particular individual and, for instance, parenting methods that were applied to him/her, often such reinforcing circumstances are "chosen" so that an existing cluster of beliefs and tendencies could be played out.

Thus it is not possible to completely protect a child from the belief systems that dominate in this reality because the entrance into this reality itself indicates that this reality must be experienced. Until a certain age parents can try to delay or lessen such an impact on child's perception by carefully choosing what the child is experiencing in the "outside world" where possible (e.g. choosing specific kindergarten, school and after-school classes) as well as setting an example for the child by acting and showing an attitude that reflects the freedom from the restrictive belief systems.

Nevertheless, also the fact that a child has parents that feel the necessity to consciously implement activities that lessen an unquestioning acceptance of delusory notions simply indicates that the particular individualized consciousness must experience such "more relaxed" circumstances. At the same time if there are parents who doesn't feel such a necessity, it means that this particular child in turn must experience different circumstances that would allow the dream scenario to realize. Therefore, in an absolute understanding there is no wrong action, irrespective of whether parents feel such a need to protect or not because the dream must express itself is it must.

Unforced and open conversation with a child about the deepest existential matters can never be harmful. However, one must remember not to make the same mistake that is often practiced by the traditional educational system – not to force already established beliefs upon a child. Instead, invite to look at everything differently, more broadly and to learn to distinguish their direct experience from ideas and concepts. If the child has an active interest in these matters and a desire to delve deeper into it, a practical approach similar to the one meant for adults can be implemented. One can practice mindfulness, raise understanding / compassion at any given situation as well as carry out evaluation of one's direct experience to recognize the illusion generated by the perception and to spot the moment at which a direct experience is turned into the mind's interpretation. While parents are practicing themselves, they may propose the child to look at something in a certain way and try to find answers within him/herself. All this should be entwined into the daily rhythm naturally and flowingly enough. And the child should always have a free choice to join or not. However, nothing is better than parents who demonstrate an understanding of the nature of this reality and "I" with their own behavior, which is not easy to accomplish of course.

Do we have a choice in awakening if everything about you or around you collapses?

Deep longing for truth, feeling this world can't be all there is and an increasing disinterest in worldly matters are symptoms of awakening, which is already happening, rather than a reason for awakening later in time. The analogy of sleep illustrates it perfectly. A person is asleep in a bed. A blanket has slipped off, and the person's body starts to feel cold. This feeling of being cold is reflected in a dream of this person. Perhaps a cold winter arrives in the dream, and the dream character starts to engage in various activities to warm itself. Obviously nothing that dream character does can alleviate the feeling of being cold because the source of this need is beyond the dream. And these dream activities started not because of some kind of a reason within the dream, but due to a greater cause outside of the dream. Only when the person wakes up, it can stop the desire for warmth by covering itself with the blanket. Similarly, the process of awakening of the particular angle or the perspective of Consciousness (that is, an individual) is reflected in this dream we call reality, as seeking for truth and doing all sorts of activities to get there.

If we ask ourselves, when exactly and how did we decide that we are now going to pursue the path towards awakening, we see that we never did. This tendency just subtly arose within us and played out like this. We are also not in charge of deciding on the level of intensity we will have for seeking the truth. For some it's higher, for some lower. Similarly, we as individuals don't produce thoughts; we experience them when they have already formed. These characters we are playing don't have a choice; however, they must believe they have because the idea of a free will is at the very base of the concept of individuality, a person. Therefore, this grand theater could not happen if this belief wasn't there.

Why do people choose to suffer?

What must be said first, the sole reason for experiencing suffering is not seeing one's true being. If one believes he/she is a person, wide array of suffering manifests out of that. When one comes to see it is the unlimited, eternal Consciousness experiencing within itself this small person, no matters of this life can shake the underlying peace. Pain still is experienced, but it no longer causes suffering.

That being said, on a relative level we see some people seem to deliberately focus on things that cause suffering, cling to thoughts and feelings that make them feel bad. In these cases we can't really say it's their choice because, although it seems we can choose what we pay attention to, what thoughts we believe in, it's not as simple as that. Truth is, most people in their everyday life reacts out of existing patterns and deeply embedded tendencies in their minds. These tendencies represent experiences that this particular angle of the Consciousness (aka a person) must live through.

What can be done to stop these tendencies? They simply must be exhausted. Usually if someone experiences that kind of mindset, but doesn't recognize it and doesn't feel something should be changed within him/herself, no one can do anything about it. It simply must exhaust itself. When that individual realizes, it has always been his/her mindset that has brought so much suffering, and longs for change, then it can be regarded as a clear symptom showing that this particular tendency has been exhausted.

What are the most common distractions encountered after undertaking the quest for enlightenment?

If one is seriously into finding the truth, then usually there are no problems regarding the intellectual side – like reading books that offer descriptions of various methods and traditions. It is not too complicated to gain a general intellectual understanding about it.

Yet, procrastination quite often arise when time comes to actually recognize and see all that by oneself, to fulfill the practical side – meditation, self-inquiry and maintaining awareness all throughout everyday life, practicing looking at ordinary situations from a different perspective.

It is the mind (which acts as a habit) that will provide all sorts of excuses to delay these activities a bit more. Thoughts arise, "I should read this book as well" or "There is a new video available. I better have a look at it."

The mind's resistance is quite a natural phenomenon. It strives to delay the end of its ruling. Often that happens by pretending that an intellectual understanding is the real thing and that it basically already is enlightenment. Thus, it keeps entertaining itself by indulging in intellectual debates about it.

True and deep longing for the truth and home will surely overcome this!

Dear reader,

Thank you for reading this book! I hope you found value in here and it was worth your time and attention. If so, I would highly appreciate if you left a review about this book on Amazon. It would certainly help other readers find it.

May you, the Consciousness, recognize yourself as yourself,
Lili

Printed in Great Britain
by Amazon